SCHIFFER PUBLISHING

4880 Lower Valley Road • Atglen, PA 19310

fashion design archive

by Zeshu Takamura

Preface

I think that students who delve into fashion can be roughly divided into three groups. First, those who love to dress fashionably. Each day, they dress themselves in a variety of stylish clothes and head out the door. This group also goes to different clothing shops, purchases new items, and enjoys wearing them around town. They simply love to purchase clothes and dress up.

Next, we have students who love to sew. Since they were very young, such students have found home economics to be their favorite subject, and they always found themselves sewing small items. Some have even sewn a dress or two by themselves. Which is to say, this group loves to create clothes.

Last, we find manga and anime enthusiasts and other artists, whose hobby is drawing pictures. Japanese anime and manga have become a worldwide cultural phenomenon, which Japan should proudly send out into the world. In recent years I have seen more and more of this type of student. They really love to draw people.

All of these students' interests can grow and allow them to pursue their place in the fashion industry. However, despite their diligent study of fashion, many of the students I have met continue to struggle to come up with original design ideas or to create their own unique designs. I try never to forget that I used to be one of them.

Those students who entered fashion school due to their love of fashion or dressmaking have far less experience in drawing designs, particularly when compared to art major students. Thus, they obviously often struggle to successfully draw designs that pop into their heads. Also, it is hard for them to grasp all the tricks needed to design unique fashions. Some of these students are so distraught that they come to consult with me directly.

Among the students who enjoy drawing pictures because of their love for manga and anime or other art, some come to me seeking advice on how to expand their range. They often feel that they lack range because they tend to draw designs that are specific to the manga and anime worlds they are accustomed to drawing.

After witnessing the struggles of these students, who are obviously trying their best to draw proper design sketches, I began to think that I should create a resource book for them. And that is the story of how this book came to be.

This book presents various methods for developing and presenting fashion design ideas. You will undoubtedly gain a wealth of fashion design know-how if you read this book all the way through, so let's begin!

—Zeshu Takamura

concepts

In this book, we will consider effective methods of conveying your ideas to others after you have come up with a fashion design. First we must determine what you need in order to come up with such a design. The necessary knowledge and skills are:

1

Clothing Structure

If you don't know the actual structure of the clothes you wish to design, all you can come up with is a vague idea. Thus, it is necessary to understand all the elements of your clothes and their design variations. Conceiving a novel design involves accumulating the conventional (i.e., designs from the past) and creating the avant-garde (i.e., new designs). The key point here is to determine how to pleasantly sabotage existing conventions.

2

Textiles (Material)

Each and every design is greatly affected by the materials used. Apparel companies determine their designs on the basis of textiles. Also, when preparing for contests, for example, making (selecting) textiles that suite your design becomes absolutely crucial. Thus, you should thoroughly understand the basics of textiles and then aim for a design that is well suited to your chosen textiles.

3

Presentation Ability

I would like to discuss unique ways of presenting your designs by expanding upon the concepts in my previous publication *Fashion Design Techniques*. Uniqueness varies by individual, so it is up to you to determine your best course of action. However, there are certain unified themes that should be adhered to when delivering impressive presentations to a third party. Let's see what we can do about those themes.

Consider the following example. I created the four designs below under the theme of "Time and Place throughout Japan."
First, I decided that each item would be a dress. Also, I created silhouettes by making the upper halves voluminous in order to emphasize the curves of the body and the flow of the dress. Exposing the legs is also part of the concept. Finally, I elected a method, called fashion croquis, to present my designs.

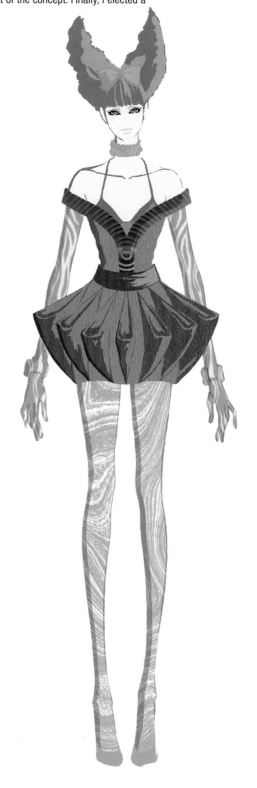

School Uniform

Many high-school girls attend classes wearing uniforms (including some whose school doesn't require them to do so), and Japanese idols use school uniforms for cosplay. These two examples show us just how much the school uniform has permeated youth culture in Japan. I designed the unique costume above on the basis of cosplay. I inverted the flared-out silhouette of a school uniform, and, by boldly rearranging the symbol of a school uniform (the sailor collar), I created a body-conscious line that is the exact opposite of a school uniform.
As far as the textile goes, I decided to use stretchable silk for the front bodice.

Origami

Origami is one of the traditional arts of Japan. By folding a piece of paper in different ways, you can create incredible three-dimensional shapes. I incorporated an origami-like design for the skirt you see above. The image for the hairstyle is that of an origami "kabuto" (war helmet) that I used to make when I was young.
I decided to go with "chirimen" (crêpe) for the textile on the front bodice.

The process for making these fashion croquis is introduced at the end of the book. I really hope you refer to that section to learn more about this crucial method of presentation.

Morning Glory

Morning glory is a garden plant popular in Japan. The petals of the morning glory have been adored by Japanese people since ancient times. Here I layered them for emphasis, and then I arranged them around the collar as a design point. I also made the legs long and thin, in the image of a crane. I chose yoryu-crêpe chiffon for the textile.

Kimono

The kimono is Japan's most iconic traditional garment. Here I made the dress length so short that the model's underwear could peek out. The balloon collar and cuffs bring out the rhythmic flow of the dress. The footwear has mixed images of kyahan (gaiters) and oiran-geta (wooden sandals) on highly exposed legs and toes.
The textile used here is "habutae" (a type of silk).

CONTENTS

Chapter 1
"Real Clothes"

What Are "Real Clothes"?

"Real clothes," meaning "clothes that are practical," are lighting up today's fashion marketplace.

They can generally be worn as "everyday clothes," and the term is used to suggest a contrast with the garments seen in fashion shows or collections that are deemed to be "too expensive to be easily purchased" or "too 'artistic' and 'designer' for daily use."
In "real clothes," functionality and design have been harmonized quite well, and they will continue to develop together in the "layered" mainstream of today, where interchangeability is key.

The History of "Real Clothes"
Let's look at how "real clothes" made it to the cutting edge of fashion.

Before the Nineteenth Century
Until the middle of the nineteenth century, the fashion industry's structure, which was very different from today, relied on a division of labor.

It was a system where the customer purchased raw fabric from a drapery shop, assembled decorative materials from a decor shop, and took the various pieces to a tailor—where the tailor created a design specific to the customer's body. A seamstress, who was separate from the tailor, was contracted to do the sewing.

That is to say, clothing design itself was not performed by a designer but rather by the customer. Also, it seems that the highest level of status in fashion at the time was not afforded to design but rather to the richness of the fabrics one used. Indeed, the art of design was not applied to the creation of garments as a whole; instead, it was a very passive, small-scale pursuit that allowed one to "design" something by adding desired decorative elements to an already accepted standard form of dress.

The Birth of *Haute Couture*
In the end it was an Englishman by the name of Charles Frederick Worth who brought about reform. After working in a London drapery shop in 1845, Charles went to France at the age of twenty. Then in 1858, he established his own couture shop. Worth, who thought the conventional fashion industry's system was inefficient, made model dresses that were already "designed," showed them to customers, took their orders, and then tailored the clothes to each customer's figure. That is how he gave birth to a more active and effective method of dressmaking. This new system became haute couture, which means "exclusive custom-fitted clothing" in French.

The couturier (designer) came to manage all aspects of the fitting process, from design to choosing textiles to revision of the finished product. Although, it should be noted that prices were quite high, and even a simple afternoon dress could cost around $1,500 (evening gowns were several times that figure). Worth, who gained prominence as the couturier (designer) to the imperial house during the reign of Napoleon III, was a hot topic at court and among the French elite, and he came to wield great power in the fashion world.

In 1868, Worth established an association of couture houses, the Chambre Syndicale de la Confection et de la Couture Pour Dames et Fillettes, which is now commonly called the Chambre Syndicale de la Haute Couture ("Trade Association of High Fashion").

In 1911, the Trade Association of High Fashion was relaunched with presentations of haute couture collections (fashion shows) twice yearly and a high level of systematization—achieved by unifying the management and creative departments and by adopting consistent operating procedures—all of which came to form the foundation of today's fashion world. Nowadays, Autumn/Winter collections come out in January and Spring/Summer collections come out in July in Paris and Rome. In 1946, there were about one hundred grand maisons, but by 2010 the total stood at only twelve, including Chanel, Dior, Givenchy, and other iconic brands. Still, today prices for haute couture fashions are very high (Chanel starts at about $20,000), and, despite the fact that customers are generally limited to a handful of multimillionaires, haute couture divisions remain because they represent a brand's influence, and it is said that they have an immense impact on the sales of prêt-à-porter fashions, perfumes, and licenses for those who participate in the presentation of haute couture collections.

The Rise of Prêt-à-porter
Haute couture is good at making liberal use of luxurious materials—in addition to high-grade cutting and sewing techniques—and it still serves its function as a place where art can be expressed through fashion. However, as a source of new trends, it has ceded its position to the next generation.

This is where prêt-à-porter comes in. Prêt-à-porter is a neologism that combines the French words "prêt," meaning "ready," and "à-porter," meaning "to wear," to indicate fashions that can be worn immediately after purchase.

Also, there is the narrow definition of "exclusive ready-to-wear," which is used by haute couture designers to distinguish their products from inferior goods. Haute couture ("exclusive custom-fitted clothing") was a long process that involved taking orders from a limited number of private customers and then constructing desired items by hand, one by one, before finally delivering them to the customer. Prêt-à-porter ("exclusive ready-to-wear") fashions involve a shorter process and are essentially mass-produced and ready for immediate sale.

The rise of youth culture is often considered to be the backdrop for the prêt-à-porter revolution. Young people in the 1960s born after World War II were in their teens and twenties, and they had enough free time and money to force their way into the middle of a cultural scene that used to be split exclusively among adults and children. Their overpowering numbers—around 50 percent of all consumers were in their late teens or early twenties—made a stir in the marketplace. Young people enjoyed fashions that were of their own choosing, and cutting-edge styles born from the culture of the streets, such as mod, psychedelic, and hippy styles and the miniskirt, began to exert pressure on the public at large. The source of new trends shifted from "the elite" to "the average youth," and fashion was popularized and began to permeate all of society. One of the things that really helped support the youth fashion movement was prêt-à-porter.

In 1959, Pierre Cardin became the first haute couture designer to present prêt-à-porter. In 1966, Yves Saint-Laurent opened a prêt-à-porter shop in the students' quarter of la Rive Gauche on the Seine River, instead of on la Rive Droite, where all of the other elite maisons were lined up. Yves Saint-Laurent, who perfectly embodied the popularization of fashion, made la Rive Gauche a major topic of discussion.

Seeing this as a new opportunity, many haute couture maisons made their full-fledged expansion into the "ready-to-wear" garment sector a reality and subsequently lent more weight to the prêt-à-porter ideal. Prêt-à-porter, which could be readily obtained if one put a little effort into it, was different from haute couture, and it received great support both from the youths who formed the core group and the general public. Then in 1973, the Trade Association of High Fashion, which had stalwartly sought to protect its traditions, established a prêt-à-porter division.

The prêt-à-porter collections that started in Paris in the 1960s are currently exhibited in five countries around the world, where fashion shows are held twice a year. Fashion shows are held six months before the actual season they represent, meaning Autumn/Winter is in March and Spring/Summer is in October. Collections are presented for one week in each of the following cities: New York, London, Milan, and Paris. One month later, they are presented in Tokyo—thus completing what are called the "five major Fashion Weeks."

It is in these fashion capitals that various prêt-à-porter brands offer their new designs, and you can be sure that makers of "real clothes" are taking notes and evolving every day. It is because of this that when we say "fashion" today, we actually mean "real clothes."

The "Real Clothes" Trend

How is the "trend" surrounding "real clothes" being created?

First of all, the direction that "color trends" will take is determined two years in advance by commissions such as Intercolor (International Commission for Color in Fashion and Textiles), which has fourteen member nations worldwide. The colors for Autumn/Winter are set in June, while those for Spring/Summer are fixed in December.

Then, a year and a half in advance, style offices in every country predict overall fashions, on the basis of colors selected by commissions such as Intercolor, and present their "trend books." In Japan, the JAFCA Fashion Color trend book is presented by the group representing Japan at Intercolor, the Japan Fashion Color Authority (JAFCA).

Next, textile trends are set. Between one and a half years and one year in advance, "yarn fairs" are staged, and yarns, selected with the previously determined color trends in mind, are placed on exhibit. Then, one year in advance, "textile trade shows" are staged, the Première Vision show in Paris being the most well known. Six months in advance, and on the basis of the information provided at yarn fairs and textile trade shows, the twice-yearly haute couture collection and prêt-à-porter collection fashion shows are held. These global-scale shows in New York, London, Milan, Paris, and Tokyo are made up of so-called Fashion Weeks.

Finally, international magazines such as *Vogue* and *Elle* analyze various fashions and explain which clothes and which styles are likely to be trendy over the next year. In Japan, this is done by magazines such as *Fashion News* (INFAS Publications), *Mode et Mode* (Mode et Mode Sha Ltd.), and *gap Press* (Gap Japan).

Some fashion show clothing can be too showy to wear around town, but I would like to reference some ways in which the ideas of fashion designers (hereafter "designers") are broken down to make street clothes. This is where all of the apparel makers who deal with "real clothes" come into play, since "real clothes" are made by apparel makers. The term "apparel" refers to clothing as a whole (garments and accessories), and the apparel makers' business consists of planning, manufacturing, and wholesaling said clothing. There are two types of apparel makers: the ones that have their own brand name, and the ones called OEM (original equipment manufacturers) that make use of another company's brand.

Designers take the concepts proposed by merchandisers (abbreviated "MD"), on the basis of trend information that changes every season (colors, textiles, silhouettes, details, and other elements that are likely to be popular), and frame their own ideas for new clothing. Designers make rough sketches of their ideas that then become so-called fashion design sketches (hereafter "design sketch"). Then, on the basis of these design sketches, the designer has a patternmaker make the necessary patterns before he creates the specifications for the garment and has a sewing factory put together the final product.

Apparel makers then put on biannual exhibitions and take orders for their products. When apparel makers hold exhibitions, information concerning trends is soon disseminated through regular domestic fashion magazines, and these trends begin to gradually circulate among consumers. Then, once the trend is established, the products are shipped by way of wholesalers to be lined up on display in stores. Since "real clothes" are born amid such high levels of specialization, there is a need for designers to have both good design sense and technical expertise, while still grasping the overall trajectory of the brand. That is also why there is a demand for designers who have the ability to communicate with many different people, who can judge the state of current world affairs, and who have a high level of sensitivity and knowledge concerning clothing.

Trends may be two years in the making, but that is not to say that all products are well received by the consumer. That is one of the great difficulties in fashion, and that is why the aforementioned SPAs (specialty store retailers of private-label apparel) succeed with their "speed." Given that they plan, develop, produce, and sell directly to consumers via company stores, they can "quickly" design, "quickly" make, and "quickly" put on display items that will sell "now." The low price and speedy development of the fashions being offered have led to this style of fashion production becoming labeled "fast fashion."

This movement has led to the devaluation of a designer's creativity. The initial stage of the movement came at the beginning of the 1990s and continued into the new millennium. Now, worldwide retail chains, such as H&M (1947/Sweden), Zara (1975/Spain), Forever 21 (1984/USA), GAP (1969/USA), Topshop (1964/Britain), and UNIQLO (1984/Japan), are all the rage. Given that up until the twentieth century product development began one to two years in advance, we can say that "fast fashion" has indeed made big waves in the fashion world.

Accordingly, there has been a rise in the number of apparel makers holding exhibitions during their targeted sales period, rather than six months in advance. The source of designers' information has changed as well. While they still pay attention to information concerning colors and materials one to two years in advance, designers also place importance on the information gleaned from fashion magazines that are currently on the stands. Thanks to this, magazines and internet sites are now using "street shots" of the clothes worn by fashionable men and women who are out and about as a good way to measure seasonal consumer trends.

In Japan, magazines such as *STREET, FRUITS*, and *TUNE* (all by *STREET* magazine) are good examples of media outlets that have focused on "street shots"—to the point where the magazines are composed almost exclusively of photographs—and forced us to question the meaning of fashion itself.

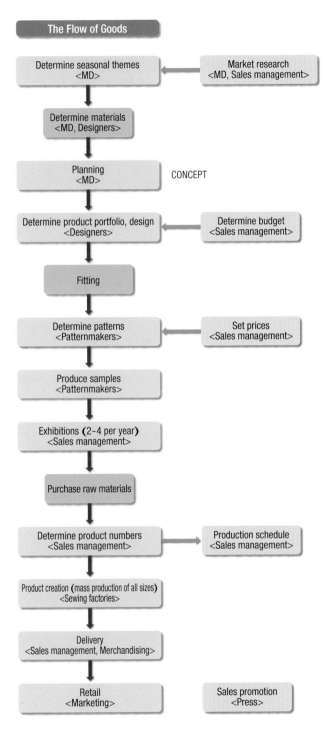

The Flow of Goods

```
Determine seasonal themes          ◄── Market research
<MD>                                    <MD, Sales management>
        │
        ▼
Determine materials
<MD, Designers>
        │
        ▼
Planning                    CONCEPT
<MD>
        │
        ▼
Determine product portfolio, design ◄── Determine budget
<Designers>                             <Sales management>
        │
        ▼
Fitting
        │
        ▼
Determine patterns                 ◄── Set prices
<Patternmakers>                         <Sales management>
        │
        ▼
Produce samples
<Patternmakers>
        │
        ▼
Exhibitions (2–4 per year)
<Sales management>
        │
        ▼
Purchase raw materials
        │
        ▼
Determine product numbers          ──► Production schedule
<Sales management>                      <Sales management>
        │
        ▼
Product creation (mass production of all sizes)
<Sewing factories>
        │
        ▼
Delivery
<Sales management, Merchandising>
        │
        ▼
Retail                                  Sales promotion
<Marketing>                             <Press>
```

Department names in brackets, MD = Merchandiser

Product Naming

Product names are applied on the basis of their place of origin (i.e., connections with a certain area, group, or sport), silhouette, individual design details, or internal characteristics. But there are also products that have multiple names.

Examples

Purpose/specific person......... Example: Pilot shirts, painter's pants, etc.

Materials, patterns................ Example: Leather jackets, plaid skirts, etc.

Details .... Example: Epaulette shirts, double-breasted jackets, etc.

Silhouette/dress length .... Example: Miniskirt, A-line dress, etc.

Products with multiple names

Materials, patterns................ Tartan

Details .... Pleats

Silhouette .... Mini

    1 Pleated skirt

    2 Plaid skirt

    3 Miniskirt

    4 Mixed (e.g., tartan miniskirt)

So, you can name an item on the basis of what you consider its main design characteristics to be. Improvements in these design characteristics have piled up over humankind's long history, and trial and error has led to the designing of stock items that many people have come to love. On the following pages, we will take a look at some of the specific design characteristics we are talking about.

Section **1** Item Variations

The purpose of "real clothes" is to have as many people as possible wear them, so comfort and simplicity are of primary importance. Therefore, "real clothes" are the basic form of an item, while the design is the more accomplished form of that item. By learning what basic forms are, you will be able to figure out what elements need to be "designed."

Types of Items and Textiles

Fabric Cloth or textiles are made from natural fibers such as cotton, linen, or silk; synthetic fibers such as polyester or nylon; or a mixture of these.
Generally, cloth doesn't stretch out when pulled, as opposed to knitted fabrics.

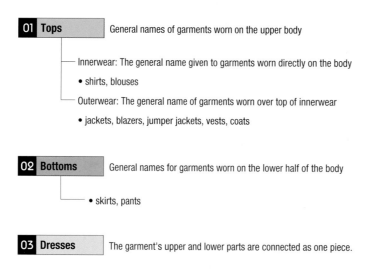

01 Tops General names of garments worn on the upper body

— Innerwear: The general name given to garments worn directly on the body
  • shirts, blouses

— Outerwear: The general name of garments worn over top of innerwear
  • jackets, blazers, jumper jackets, vests, coats

02 Bottoms General names for garments worn on the lower half of the body
  • skirts, pants

03 Dresses The garment's upper and lower parts are connected as one piece.

Knitwear The general name of garments made from knit fabrics. Since the fabric is stretchy, it is easier to make garments fit the body without relying on structural lines. Other terms: jersey.

04 Knitwear The general name of garments made from knit fabrics
  • sweaters, cut-and-sew, and others

05 Underwear Undergarments. For material, many use knit fabrics, but some use cloth.
  • brassieres, shorts

01 Item Variations: Tops

Shirts

"Shirt" is a catchall term for a garment worn on the upper body. The shirt developed as a male garment. It is also worn as innerwear, such as a tank top, or in some cases it can be outerwear made from thick fabric.

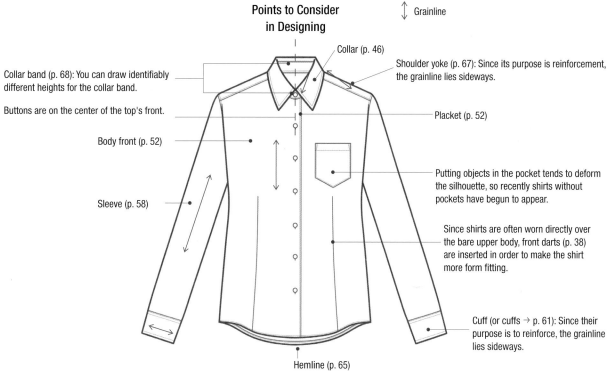

Points to Consider in Designing

Grainline

Collar (p. 46)

Collar band (p. 68): You can draw identifiably different heights for the collar band.

Shoulder yoke (p. 67): Since its purpose is reinforcement, the grainline lies sideways.

Buttons are on the center of the top's front.

Placket (p. 52)

Body front (p. 52)

Putting objects in the pocket tends to deform the silhouette, so recently shirts without pockets have begun to appear.

Sleeve (p. 58)

Since shirts are often worn directly over the bare upper body, front darts (p. 38) are inserted in order to make the shirt more form fitting.

Cuff (or cuffs → p. 61): Since their purpose is to reinforce, the grainline lies sideways.

Hemline (p. 65)

1 Regular Shirt
The general name for plain shirts. They have simple designs with only the necessities such as the collar, body front, sleeves, and cuffs. Other terms: dress shirt, plain shirt.

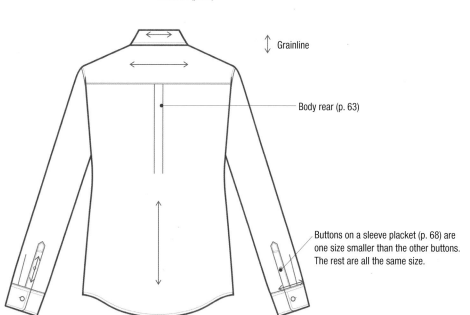

Grainline

Body rear (p. 63)

Buttons on a sleeve placket (p. 68) are one size smaller than the other buttons. The rest are all the same size.

2 Ivy Shirt

These shirts commonly employ Ivy League styles. They have front-panel plackets, button-down collars, and a button attached in the middle at the back of the collar. The fabric used is colored, nonpatterned oxford cloth, gingham, or Madras plaid broad cloth. Other terms: button-down shirt (BD shirt).

3 Safari Shirt

These shirts are usually worn on hunting trips to Africa. Their special features are epaulets, patches, flap pockets, and a belt.

4 Shirt Bodysuit

A shirt that also covers the crotch, which can be fastened and unfastened. No matter how you move, it follows your movements. Many of them use stretch fabric.

Blouse

A catchall term for women's shirts

1 Regular Blouse

While accommodating various styles, blouses can be tailored to fit the curves of the female body by utilizing gathers and drapes.

2 Cache Coeur

This blouse wraps around the body without using buttons. Other term: wrap blouse.

3 Tunic

A cylinder silhouette blouse. Tunic means "underwear" in Latin.

4 Tiered Cami (Camisole)

Spaghetti straps expose the shoulders. Sleeveless women's tops. The majority of camis use thin fabric. Originally, the cami was considered lingerie, but recently it has become more of a blouse. Long camis are also called camisole dresses.

Jacket

Jackets are garments worn on the upper body, such as tailored suit jackets.

1 Tailored Jacket (single-breasted)
Single-breasted, tailored suit jacket

Design Features

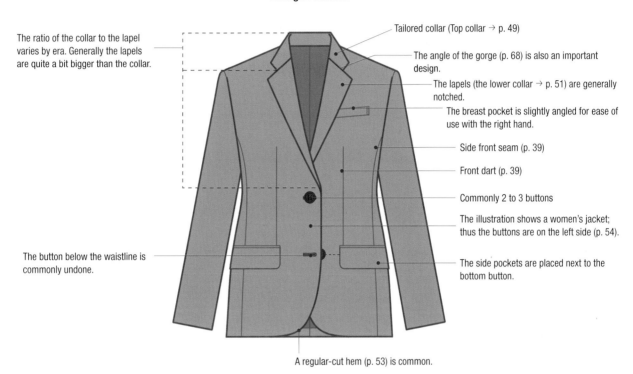

The ratio of the collar to the lapel varies by era. Generally the lapels are quite a bit bigger than the collar.

Tailored collar (Top collar → p. 49)

The angle of the gorge (p. 68) is also an important design.

The lapels (the lower collar → p. 51) are generally notched.

The breast pocket is slightly angled for ease of use with the right hand.

Side front seam (p. 39)

Front dart (p. 39)

Commonly 2 to 3 buttons

The illustration shows a women's jacket; thus the buttons are on the left side (p. 54).

The button below the waistline is commonly undone.

The side pockets are placed next to the bottom button.

A regular-cut hem (p. 53) is common.

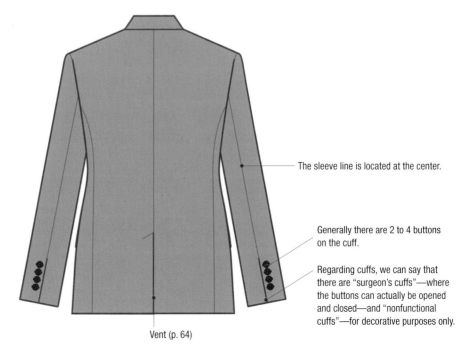

The sleeve line is located at the center.

Generally there are 2 to 4 buttons on the cuff.

Regarding cuffs, we can say that there are "surgeon's cuffs"—where the buttons can actually be opened and closed—and "nonfunctional cuffs"—for decorative purposes only.

Vent (p. 64)

2 Tailored Jacket (double-breasted)

Double-breasted tailored suit jacket. They commonly have a peaked lapel, four to six buttons, and a square-cut hem.

3 Shooting Jacket

A type of sports jacket originally worn for hunting. Design features include gun patches (p. 69), elbow patches (p. 69), and throat tabs (p. 69). Other terms: hunting jacket.

4 Norfolk Jacket

A type of sports jacket. A shooting jacket originally worn as a hunting garment by the Duke of Norfolk in England. This jacket's impractical design, filled with its country taste, is quite interesting. Design features include two vertical panes attaching the shoulders to the side pockets and the waist belt.

5 Collarless Jacket

A general term for jackets without a collar. The illustration is a tweed, rounded-neck jacket. This particular style is called a Chanel jacket. Its trimming has a quite distinctive design.

6 Spencer Jacket

A type of short-length jacket. Its name originated with Earl Spencer from England, who originally wore this type of jacket. Pointed front hem (p. 65).

7 Peplum Jacket

A jacket in which the peplum (p. 65) creates its distinctive design

Blazer

Blazers are tailored sport jackets first created in England. The distinctive elements of blazers include metal buttons, patch pockets (p. 73), and emblems (p. 69). The material used in blazers is flannel.

1 Traditional Blazer

Navy-blue flannel, natural shoulders (p. 56), single-breasted triple buttons (p. 54), and gold buttons create the traditional blazer's distinctive look. Other terms: Ivy blazer, Brooks model.

2 School Blazer

This blazer is so called because of its use in school uniforms. Gold buttons and an emblem create a distinctive look. As we can see from this illustration, some blazers have trim (p. 69).

3 Club Blazer

This blazer comes from uniforms used at sports clubs in England. Its distinctive look is created through the use of emblems and club stripes (striped patterns developed around club colors).

Jumper

The general term for waist-length jackets. This type of garment is supposed to be worn when one moves actively, such as during sports, work, or outdoor activities. Thus, many of them are designed while paying great attention to functionality.
Other terms: blouson, short jacket

1 Rider Jacket
A type of leather jumper for bikers.
Other term: motorcycle jacket.

2 Denim Jacket
A waist-length jacket made of denim. Originally it was used as a type of pullover-style work clothing. However, it has become tight fitting and highly functional as its style metamorphosed. Other term: jean jacket.

3 Down Jacket
A waist-length jacket that is padded with feathers and uses mainly nylon fabric

4 N-3
A jacket developed by the US Air Force for use in extremely cold regions. The N-3A is Air Force blue, while the N-3B is sage green.

5 Letterman Jacket (Baseball Jacket)
Originally letterman jackets were bench wear for baseball players. At present they have become street fashion items among youths.

Vest

Sleeveless waist-length garment worn over shirts, etc.
Other terms: gilet, waistcoat

1 Regular Vest
General term for vests. Commonly single-breast with a pointed front.

2 Odd Vests
A spare vest. Defining characteristics include a casual look and being constructed with fabrics that are different from the suit. Other term: fancy vest.

3 Knit Vests
Commonly they are V-neck, and the sleeves and hem are rib-stitched.

4 Long Gilet

5 Down Vest
Feather-padded vest

Coat

The outermost garment, sleeved and long in length. Lengths above the knee are called short coats, knee-length styles are half coats, and below-the-knee coats are termed overcoats or long coats.

1 Peacoat (Pea Jacket)

This garment was originally a short coat worn on battleships in the British navy, which then spread to the population in general. "Pea" is simply the name of the material used in the original coats. At present, the material is a navy-blue Melton fabric. This coat's distinctive look is created through its six buttons, double breast, and muff pockets (p. 74). Other terms: watch coat, bridge coat, pilot coat.

2 Trench Coat

Originally a coat developed by the British army during World War I for trench warfare. It is a highly functional garment whose various design details have the express purpose of being functional. Burberry and Aquascutum trench coats are well known. The waterproofing cotton gabardine "Burberry" is the most common material for these coats.

3 Cape

This is a sleeveless outer garment that covers everything from the shoulders to the lower back. Outer garments that cover everything down to the lower body are called cloaks, not capes.

4 Duffle Coat

A thick wool half coat with a hood (p. 70) and toggle fasteners (p. 70). Duffle is the name of a town in Belgium. It is also the name of the wool fabric manufactured in that town. Originally these coats were used by workers; however, they gained rapidly in popularity after the British navy adopted them during World War II.

5 Cape Coat

A coat with a cape

02 Item Variations: Bottoms

Skirt

General term for a tube-shaped garment that covers from the waist down both legs, but without separating the legs

1 Flare Skirts

A skirt that has volume from the hip to the hem, with natural waves. It has anywhere from one to eight gores.

Points to Consider when Designing

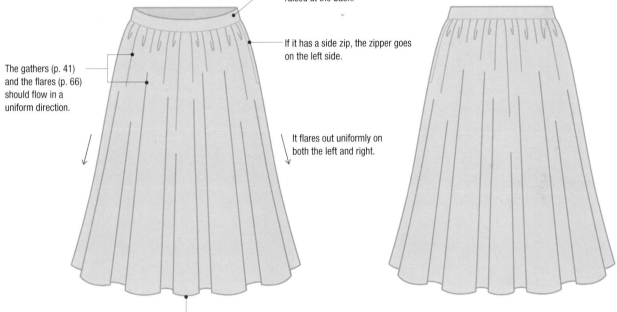

The gathers (p. 41) and the flares (p. 66) should flow in a uniform direction.

In many skirts the waistband (p. 40) drops down at the front and is raised at the back.

If it has a side zip, the zipper goes on the left side.

It flares out uniformly on both the left and right.

The flares make a wavelike line.

2 Pleated Skirts

A general term for a skirt with pleats (p. 71)

3 Tiered Skirts

A skirt with tiers (p. 66) or horizontal layers, one to eight gores

4 Circle Skirts

When this skirt is spread out, it makes a circular shape. Since the skirt is sewn by joining fabrics in a circular shape, it makes very beautiful wavy flares when hanging down.

5 Gypsy Skirts

This skirt is quite long and has different designs: plenty of gathers, two or three layers, lots of frills, etc.

6 Escargot Skirts (Bias-Cut Skirts)

A skirt sewn in a spiral shape, similar to the shape of snail's shell, by joining bias-cut fabric. There is also a wrap skirt type. Other term: spiral skirt.

7 Gored Skirts

A skirt with gores (p. 72). A type of flare skirt, spreading out at the hem, with the number of gores ranging from two to eight.

8 Yoke-Waist Skirts

A skirt that has a yoke around the waist

9 Skirt-on-Skirt

A skirt overlapping another skirt

10 Prairie Skirts

A skirt flaring at the bottom, with a yoke at the hipline

11 Suspender Skirts

The skirt is suspended from the shoulders with a pair of suspenders that are attached at the waist.

12 Pareos

Pareos are originally Tahitian traditional costumes. In Tahitian the word "pareos" means "a skirt that wraps around." Pareos are known for their vibrant patterns and colors and are sized around 90 cm x 180 cm (35$\frac{1}{2}$″ x 70$\frac{7}{8}$″). Wrap the pareos around the hip and tie its ends to make a skirt. Usually worn over swimwear. Other term: sarong.

13 Wraparound Culottes

Though the wraparound culotte looks like a pair of short pants from the rear, from the front it appears to be a wraparound skirt. It appeared during the Victorian era, in the late nineteenth century, to allow women to ride a horse. Other term: skort.

14 Culottes

Although the culotte flares at the hem and looks like a skirt, it has separate legs like a pair of pants.

Pants

General term for a garment that covers both legs separately. Synonyms: trousers (pants that are usually paired with a jacket to make a suit), slacks (a spare pair of pants not paired with a jacket), pantaloons.

Points to Consider when Designing

The front zipper and button are not located dead center.

Bar tacks (p. 72) are also an important part of the design.

This illustration shows the right front.

The fly does not reach to the inseam.

The back pockets (p. 75) are not visible from the front, so their openings can be left loosely open.

The leather patch is an important element of design.

Be sure to draw inseams. Do not cut corners.

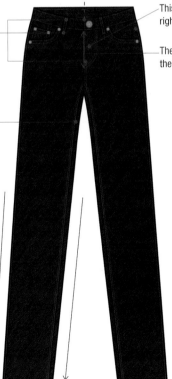

1 Jeans

Jeans are twilled denim fabric pants. The word "denim" comes from the French "serge de Nîmes," which became de nime, and then denim. Serge is a French twilled fabric produced in Nîmes, France. Other term: blue jeans.

The silhouette and the width of the bottom create different styles.

2 Painter Pants
Painters' workpants

3 Cargo Pants
Thick and durable cotton workpants
worn by workers on freight vessels

4 Sarouel Pants
Traditional Islamic clothes. The drooped
crotch makes up the key element in the
sarouel pants' unique design.

5 Jodhpurs Pants
A type of horse-riding pant with a
distinctive flared silhouette above
the knee

6 Gaucho Pants
Loose, flared-bottom, three-quarter-length
pants that are worn by cowboys in the
prairie regions of South America

7 Knickerbockers (Knickers)
Sportswear primarily worn outdoors.
Knee-length trousers with buckle-
fastened bottoms. Flannel or tweed is
commonly used for knickerbockers.

8 Shorts
General term used for short-length pants

9 Pumpkin Pants
Pants that have a pumpkin-like silhouette

10 Harem Pants
Worn by Muslim women. Balloon-shaped pants with
a tight hem. Also seen in Indian traditional clothing.
Other terms: Indian pants, balloon pants.

11 Zouave Pants
From the waist to the hem, these pants have plenty of
gathers and a narrowed hem. Originated as uniforms worn
by Algerian infantry recruited by the French army in 1830.

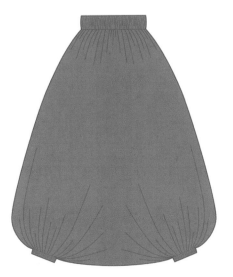

12 Flying-Squirrel Pants
As the name implies, these pants have a flying-
squirrel silhouette. Other term: Aladdin pants.

Dresses

A garment that covers the body, in one piece, from the waist upward and downward

2 Shirt Dress
A one-piece garment tailored like a shirt

1 One-Piece Dress
A woman's garment that has both the bodice
and skirt attached. As far as one-piece
lingerie is concerned, long items are called
"negligee," while shorter items, paired with
shorts, are called "baby dolls."

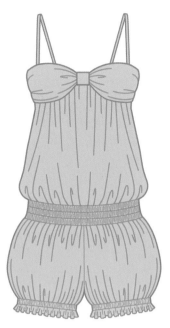

3 Combinaison
A one-piece bodice to which sleeves and pants are attached. In English, it is called "a combination." The illustration shows a "romper." Originally the romper was baby clothing.
Other term: jumpsuits (one-piece work clothes).
*The all-in-one is a type of lingerie that functions as a brassiere, girdle, and corset together. Also called a bodysuit.

4 Salopette Skirt
A salopette bottom is a skirt.

5 Salopette
The salopette has pants, or a skirt, attached to a bib-and-brace. There is no fabric over the back. "Salopette" means "work clothes worn to protect one from getting dirty." The origin of the word is from the French salope ("getting dirty" or "dirty"). In English, they are usually called overalls.

6 Jumper Dress
The bodice and skirt are attached to each other. The shape is something like a sleeveless one-piece skirt. The jumper is never worn by itself. It always goes over a blouse, shirt, sweater, or other top.

Item Variations: Knitwear

Knitwear

General term used for knitted garments

Sweater — Knitwear tops

1 Pullover
A sweater worn by pulling it over one's head. Sometimes the pullover is simply called a sweater.

2 Cardigan
Open-front sweater

3 Knitwear Dress
If the length is longer, you get a dress.

Cut-and-Sew Knitwear — General term for garments that are made of jersey material that can be cut and sewn

1 T-shirt
Collarless shirts. The name originated with the T-shape made by the shirt when both sleeves are spread out. Originally the T-shirt was used as innerwear, but after the 1950s it gradually became outerwear.

2 Tank Top
Sleeveless with a neckline that is either wide or deep

3 Cami (Camisole)
Camis (other than those that are cut-and-sew) make use of glossy and sheer material such as polyester, nylon, georgette, or tulle (p. 14).

4 Leggings
Pants, similar to tights, that fit snugly around the legs

5 Stirrup Pants (Stirrup Leggings)
There is a band worn under the arch of the foot.

(**Sweatshirts**)

A type of cut-and-sew knitwear made of brushed-back cotton jersey. Has superior movability, sweat absorbency, and protection against cold.

1 Pullover
Among sweatshirts, the pullover is synonymous with sports clothing. Other term: sweatshirt.

2 Hoodie (Hooded Sweatshirt)
A sweatshirt with a hood

Others

1 Track Jackets
A catchall term for knitwear that is elastic due to its use of knit fabric (jersey). Since jersey is elastic and movable, it is often used for sports uniforms and athletic attire. The word "jersey" comes from the fabric used in fisherman's work clothes on England's Jersey Channel Island. Other terms: training jacket, warm-up jacket.

Underwear

Undergarments. Sometimes distinguished as lingerie or underwear. Most underwear uses knit fabric, but some uses cloth.

Brassiere An undergarment adjusted to the shape of the breasts

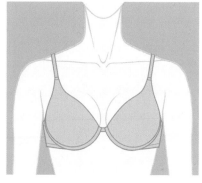

1 Seamless Bra
There are no seams (stitches) on the cups. Convenient when wearing thin clothes.

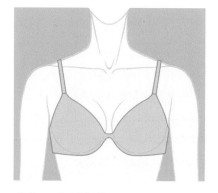

2 Concealed-Wire Bra
The stitches around the underwire are invisible on the surface of the cups. They look like a bikini top and are convenient when wearing thin clothes (similar to seamless bras).

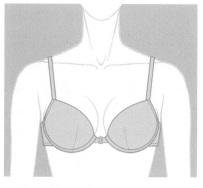

3 Front-Closure Bra
Also called front-hook bras. Secured with a front hook so that the backline remains clean and beautiful.

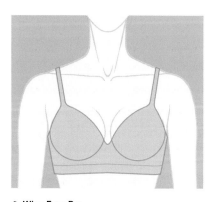

4 Wire-Free Bra
These bras have no wire and are therefore quite comfortable to wear. They are quite suitable for exercising.

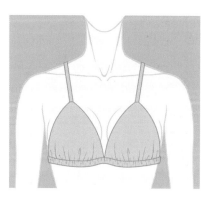

5 Bralette
No wire. Bikini-like design.

6 Bustier
Covers the torso. Sometimes used as outerwear.

Brassiere Design Variations

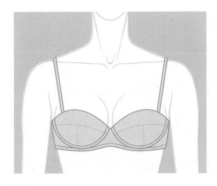

1 Demi-cup
Demi means half. As its name suggests, this bra covers half of the breast and lifts it up, all while forcing the breasts into a rounded shape.

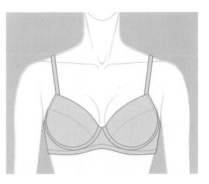

2 Three-Quarter-Cup Bra
The top quarter of the cup is cut diagonally from side to center. Pushes the breasts up and makes them look more compact.

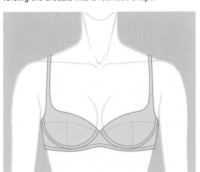

3 Shelf-Cup Bra
Lifts the breasts up and holds them in a shelflike cup. Since this bra lifts the breasts nicely, it is particularly suited to breasts that sag.

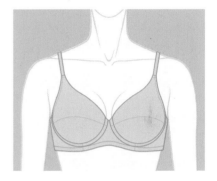

4 Full-Support (Full-Cup)
Completely wraps around the breasts. Provides maximum support so the breasts don't jiggle.

Strap Variations

Straps: shoulder straps

1 Regular
The most common type of strap. It extends to the side belt from the top of the cup.

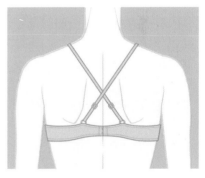

2 Crisscross
These straps cross at the back.

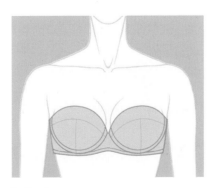

3 Strapless
No straps

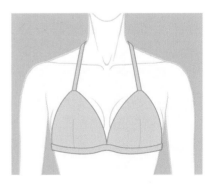

4 Halter
The backline is more sleek and beautiful because the straps are wrapped around the neck.

Shorts/Underpants/Panties   Underwear that covers the bottom

1 Thong (G-string)
The front is in a bikini style, while the buttocks remain uncovered. This is also the so-called T-back style.

2 String Bikini
A bikini-style piece of underwear with side strings

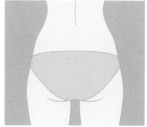

3 Bikini
The most basic type. The name comes from the bikini, a two-piece swimsuit.

4 Hipster
In between a bikini and boyshorts. These panties don't creep up to the base of the legs.

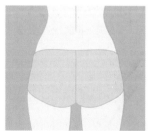

5 Boy Shorts
The hem is horizontal, much like a man's boxers. These shorts provide a certain sense of security.

6 Tap Pants
Flared at the bottom and highly fashionable

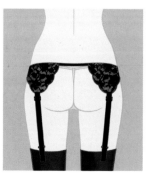

7 Garter Belt
A belt that has attachments for hanging stockings

8 Drawers
A knee-length undergarment. Often used in Lolita fashions.

Hipline Design Variations

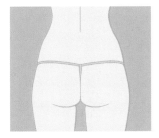

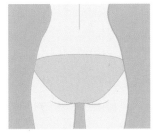

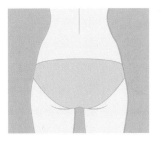

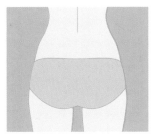

1 Thong
No need to be concerned with panty lines here. The roundness of the buttocks is nicely displayed with this type of underwear.

2 Bikini
Covers ³/₄ of the hips and makes them look compact

3 American
The lower hips become visible.

4 Full Cover
Snugly covers the buttocks

Girdle Design Variations

The girdle is an undergarment for "shaping" the lower body.

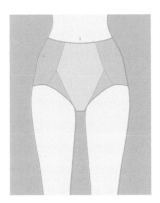

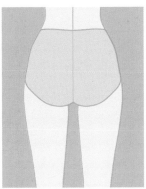

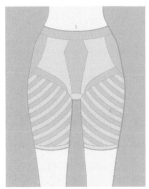

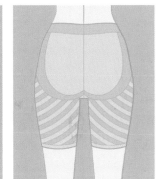

1 Short Girdle
Short length, panty-like, girdle

2 Soft Girdle
This type of girdle is made from pantyhose material, which gives it a soft texture. These girdles have excellent shaping abilities because of the complex weaving techniques used to make them.

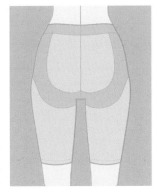

3 Long Girdle
Long in length and used to "shape up" everything from the belly to the thighs

Section 2
Design Variations

Silhouette

The silhouette is the overall form of a garment. The three key points to creating a garment's form are the **length** (length = vertical balance) that covers the body, the **outline** (volume = horizontal balance), and the **structural lines** that create the outline.

Outline: structural lines; other term: form

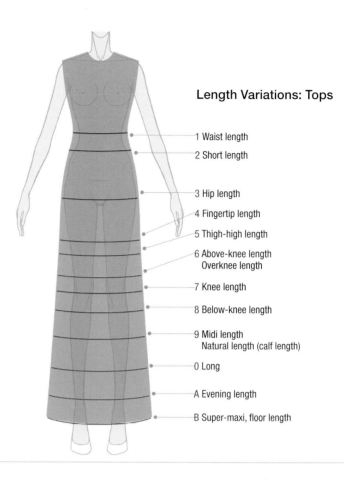

Length Variations: Tops

1 Waist length
2 Short length
3 Hip length
4 Fingertip length
5 Thigh-high length
6 Above-knee length
 Overknee length
7 Knee length
8 Below-knee length
9 Midi length
 Natural length (calf length)
0 Long
A Evening length
B Super-maxi, floor length

Outline Variations

1 A-line
The silhouette flares out at the hem, thus making the shape of a capital "A." First introduced by Christian Dior at his 1955 Spring/Summer collection, the A-line has now become a standard silhouette. Other terms: tent-line, trapeze-line, pyramid-line, triangle-line (includes the inverted triangle-shape silhouette).

2 Shift Line
A shift is a form of underwear called a chemise. Like a chemise, it has a slim silhouette that flows straight down from the shoulder.

3 I-line
A slender and elongated silhouette, much like the letter "I."
Other term: pencil-line.

4 Sheath Line
The silhouette fits tightly on the body, as if it were a sheath for holding a sword.

5 Straight Line
A straight-line type silhouette.
Other terms: box-line (a box-shaped silhouette), rectangular-line.

6 Sack Line
This silhouette is slightly loose fitting and flows straight down like a sack.

7 H-line

Similar to a capital "H," this is a slim silhouette that fits loosely around the waist. The horizontal line in the letter "H" is created through the use of a belt or a seam on the waistline. Christian Dior first introduced this silhouette at his Fall/Winter Collection in 1954.

8 Princess Line

By specifically using a vertical panel line (a seam line) to tighten the waistline, thus creating a tight-fitting image, this silhouette gently flares out from the hip to hemline. Since the panel line itself is also called a princess line, the silhouette may also be called a princess silhouette. Princess-line dresses were adored by Empress Alexandra—the wife of early-twentieth-century British king Edward VII—during her princess era.

9 Figure 8

This silhouette looks like a number "8" and was introduced by Christian Dior at his Paris Collection debut 1947 Spring/ Summer Collection. This silhouette emphasizes femininity and is characterized by a sloped shoulder, small waist (called a "bee's hip"), and a midlength (p. 36) flared skirt. Other terms: the New Look, Carolle.

10 Fit & Flare Line

The upper part of the body is fitted, while the rest of the dress flares out from waistline to hemline. Other terms: fit & swing line, tight & flare line.

11 X-line

This silhouette creates an "X"-like shape. Flared out at the bottom, this silhouette is characterized by a broad shoulder line and small waist.

12 V-line

Shaped like the letter "V," this silhouette is like an inverted triangle where the broad shoulder line narrows down toward the hemline. Other term: wedge line.

13 Y-line

Like a shape of the letter "Y." Broad shouldered and narrow toward the waist, thus creating a slender silhouette from the waist to the hem.

14 Body-Conscious Line

This silhouette fits tightly to the body.
Other terms: slim line, bandage line (tightly fitted like a wrapped bandage), body-figure line.

15 Tulip Line

A silhouette that is similar in shape to a tulip. Characterized by a gently sloped shoulder line and a plump chest area, this silhouette also has a small waist and a stemlike shaped skirt. Christian Dior introduced this silhouette at his 1953 Spring/Summer Collection.

16 Pegtop Line

This is a silhouette that swells like a cask in the middle and then intensely narrows toward the hem. This line was introduced at Christian Dior's last collection, the 1975 Fall/ Winter Collection.
Other terms: spindle line (Dior's last collection, 1975 Fall/Winter), baril line (meaning a barrel-like shape).

17 Eggshell Line

This silhouette is rounded, like the shape of an egg. Other term: oval line.

18 Mermaid Line

A silhouette that looks like a mermaid. It fits tightly from below the knees up to the hipline. The hem flares, making this dress look like a fishtail.

Outline Variations

1 Tight Line
An outline that is fitted from waist to hip

2 Cocoon Line
An outline that is rounded at the hips

3 Straight Line
A linear outline. Other terms: box line, rectangular line.

4 A-line
An outline that flares out like an "A"

5 Flare Line
An outline that widens toward the hem, making a wavy hemline

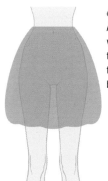

6 Balloon
A puffed and voluminous outline that gathers in at the hemline like a balloon

7 Peg-top Line
Loosely fits around the hips and becomes tight toward the hem.

8 Mermaid Line
An outline that looks like a mermaid. Fitted to the knee and flares out to the hem.

Length Variations: Skirts

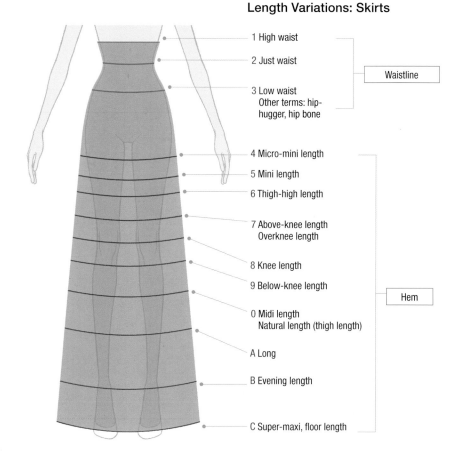

1 High waist

2 Just waist

3 Low waist
Other terms: hip-hugger, hip bone

Waistline

4 Micro-mini length

5 Mini length

6 Thigh-high length

7 Above-knee length
Overknee length

8 Knee length

9 Below-knee length

0 Midi length
Natural length (thigh length)

A Long

B Evening length

C Super-maxi, floor length

Hem

Length Variations: Pants

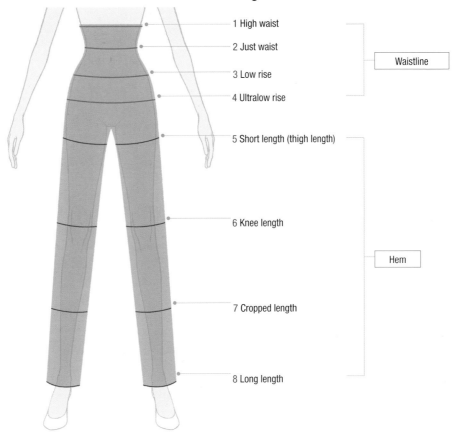

1 High waist
2 Just waist
3 Low rise
4 Ultralow rise

Waistline

5 Short length (thigh length)

6 Knee length

Hem

7 Cropped length

8 Long length

Outline Variations

1 Slim Line
A slender line fitted to the legs

2 Straight Line
A line that is straight from the hips to the hem

3 Pegtop Line
This outline has a deep front rise and wide hips. It becomes intensely narrow toward the hem. Other terms: buggy top, wide-slim pants.

4 Baggy Line
Widens intensely from the hips to the hem. Other term: bag wide pants.

5 Flare Line
Gently flares out from the hips or the thigh toward the hem

6 Bell Bottom
A kind of flared pant that is fitted down to the knees and then flares out like a bell below the knees

Structural Line

When using flat fabric to create the roundness and puffiness that is associated with the human body, it is necessary to take in portions of fabric here and there. Also, several pieces of fabric must be sewn together. Seams are created as a result of these requirements. These seams are called structural lines.

Structural Line: Tops

Front Style

In order to cover the swell of the chest and the narrow waist, structural lines are necessary.

Inner

Darts: The part of the fabric that is taken in and sewn down. Darts run from anywhere on the body toward the bust point.

1 Front Dart
Runs from near the center to the bust point

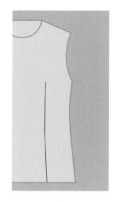

2 Waist Dart
Runs from the waistline to the bust point

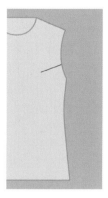

3 Armhole Dart
Runs from the armhole to the bust point

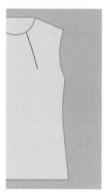

4 Neckline Dart
Runs from the neckline to the bust point

5 Side Dart
Runs from a side line to the bust point

6 Shoulder Dart
Runs from the shoulder line to the bust point

Panel Line: Seam Line

7 Common Panel Line
Refers to the side of the body

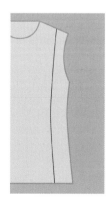

8 Princess Line
A vertical panel line

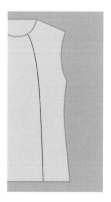

9 Princess Line Variation

10 Heart-Shaped Panel Line

11 High-Waist Panel Line

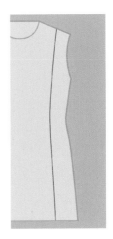
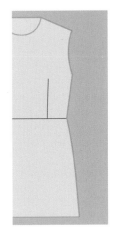

Outer

1 Panel Line

2 Dart and Panel Line
Commonly, the dart stops at the pocket. Does not go through to the hem.

3 Princess Line

4 Waist Seamline

Back Style
The panel is relatively simple, and so is the structural line.

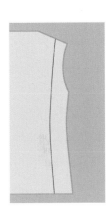

Inner

1 Dart

2 Dart

3 Princess Line

4 Panel Line

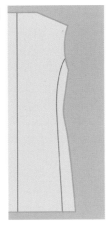

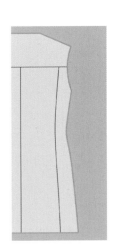

Outer

1 Back Seam and Panel Line

2 Back Seam and Princess Line

3 Back Seam and Panel Line on Yoke

4 Back Seam and Princess Line on Yoke

Structural Line: Bottoms

Waistline

Waistband

Belt-like fabric around the waist of a set of bottoms

1 Separate Waistband
Separated from the bodice

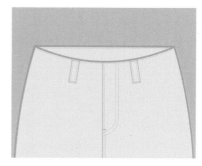

2 One-Piece Waistband
Attached to a bodice.
Other terms: California waistband, continuous.

Fly

1 Fly Front
Opening in the front (refer p. 52 for fly front)

Zip Fly
Zipped up

Button Fly
Buttoned up

2 Side Opening
Usually it is the left side that is open. Many of these bottoms have covered zippers (refer to p. 67 for covered zippers).

3 Back Opening

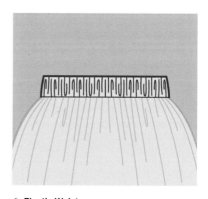

4 Elastic Waist
The waist is elastic, making these bottoms easy to put on and pull off.

Fronts

1 Darts
A piece of excess fabric that is folded and sewn down in order to add shape

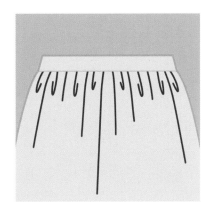

2 Gathers
Created by sewing together a loose row of stitches. Since gathers are simply sewn stitches, their folds disappear toward the hem. Commonly the gathers are on the front and back of a bodice and skirt.

3 Panel
A piece of fabric that makes up a skirt. Usually even numbers of panels—such as four, six, or eight—are used to make a skirt.

 Pleats

Folding fabric creates a pleat. Compared to gathers, we can say that each folded line makes an acute angle. Generally, pleats are on the front and back of a bodice and pants.

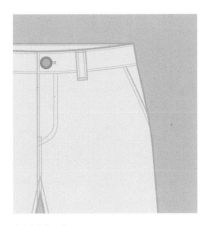

4 Flat Front
Without pleats.
Other term: plain front.

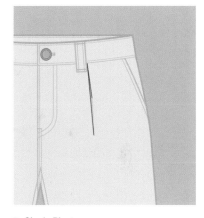

5 Single Pleat
Only one pleat

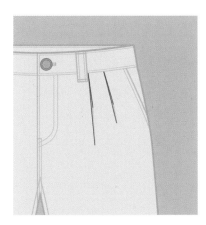

6 Double Pleats
Two pleats

7 Inside Pleat
A pleat that is folded inward. Usually the pleat is folded outward and is called an outside pleat.

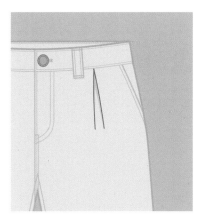

8 Inverted Pleat
A pleat made by inverting a box pleat

Parts

A general term for any element that makes up a garment

Tops: Parts

Neckline

The line around the neck on a bodice. There are abundant variations because neckline designs surround the face and are very noticeable. Can simply be called "the neck."

Round Neck

1 Round Neck
Generally this term refers to all rounded necks. However, in the narrow sense, it is either the line that follows along the base of the neck or the line that exposes the collarbone.

2 Crew Neck
Closely touches the base of the neck. It is smaller than a round neck.

3 Henry Neck
This is a type of round neck that opens at the front and buttons up. Usually it has two to three buttons.

High Neck

In the broader sense of the term, a "high neck" is a catchall term for a neckline where the fabric of the bodice stands up around the neck.

15 High Neck
In the narrow sense, this is a stand-up collar that is 2 to 3 cm (¾" to 1¼") tall. They do not fold.

16 Turtleneck
The neckline is folded double or triple.

17 Mock Turtleneck
There are no folds and the collar is taller than a high neck.

18 Funnel Neck
A cylindrical shaped neckline that is elongated upward like a funnel

19 Bottleneck
A neckline that stands up along the neck like the mouth of a bottle

20 Rolled Neck
A collar that is naturally rolled up

21 Standing Neck
A neckline standing away from the neck

Low Neckline

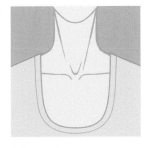

4 U-neckline
Shaped like a capital letter "U," this neckline has vertical depth.

5 Oval Neckline
This is a neckline that is elongated vertically, like an egg.

6 Oblong Neckline
A neckline that is elongated horizontally. This could also be called an oval neckline.

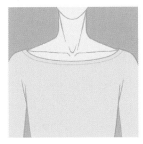

7 Boat Neck
A wide neckline that is similar to the shape of a boat.
Other term: bateau neckline.

8 Off-the-Shoulder
A neckline that exposes the shoulders

9 Scoop Neckline
This neckline is shaped like it was scooped out with a shovel. It is deeper than a boat neck.

V-neck

A general term for necklines that are cut in the shape of a "V"

10 Regular V-neck
The most common neckline. Often simply called a V-neck.

11 V-neck Cardigan
The front lap of a cardigan that makes a V shape

12 Crossover V-neck
The corner of the V-neck is crossed.

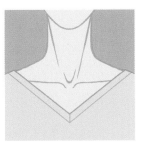

13 V-shape Crew Neck
The angle of the V-neck is extremely shallow. One with a deep angle is called "deep V-neck."
Other terms: highest V-neck, angled crew neck.

14 Spoon Neck
A neckline shaped like the scoop of a spoon. This neck has a shape somewhere between the V-line and the U-neck.

Other Necklines

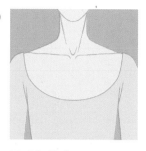

22 *Décolleté*
Décolleté is a French word that represents the part of the body from the neck to the chest. Thus, this is a neckline that emphasizes the décolleté image by using a low neckline and exposing the cleavage.

23 Keystone Neck
A variation of the V-neck without the sharp angle.
Other term: squared V-neck.

24 Square Neck
A neckline where the base of the neckline is squared off

25 Rectangular Neck
A square neck that is elongated horizontally

26 Diamond Neck
Shaped like a diamond, this neckline can either be cut like a triangle or a pentagon.

27 Keyhole Neckline
A neckline that is cut like a keyhole

28 Plunging Neck
A round neckline that has a sharp V shape cut into it

29 Heart-Shaped Neck
A neckline that is cut like the bottom portion of a heart shape

30 Sweetheart Neckline
A heart-shaped-type neckline, but with a deeper and wider heart shape

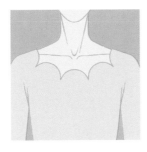

31 Scalloped Neckline
A neckline that imitates the wavy shape of a scallop shell

32 Halter Neckline
A neckline that hangs from the neck with straps or fabric that is attached to a bodice. The back is largely exposed.

33 Camisole Neck
Shoulder straps hold in position this neckline, which is cut horizontally at the bust line. There are many variations of this particular neckline.

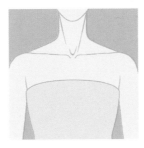

34 Strapless Neckline
Without shoulder straps

35 Oblique Neckline
A neckline that cuts diagonally from one shoulder to under the opposite arm.
Other terms: one-shoulder neckline, asymmetric neckline.

36 Cowl Neckline
A neckline with rounded folds

37 Drawstring Neckline
A neckline that can be tightened with a drawstring

38 Crossed Shawl Collar
Crossed shawl/scarf collar. The name is derived from the fact that it appears as if the model is wearing a scarf.

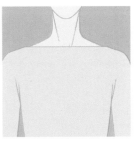

39 Slashed Neckline
Cuts straight across the neck

Collar: General term for designs around the neckline. For tailored collars, the term usually refers to the top collar.

Collars of Shirts and Blouses

Spread Collar

This collar consists of a collar band (p. 68) and a collar leaf (p. 68).
Other term: two-piece collar.

1 Regular Collar
The most basic shirt collar

2 Button-Down Collar (B.D.)
A collar that must be fastened with a button. John Brooks, grandson of a Brooks Brothers founder (leaders of Ivy League style), initially commercialized the button-down collar based on an idea that came to him when he examined shirts worn by British polo players. These shirts became a must-have item for anyone who wanted to portray Ivy League style.

3 Contrast Collar
Left: The collar and cuffs are plain white, but other parts are either striped or plain white.
Right: This is the style where only the collar is plain white.

4 Arched Collar
A collar with arched (lengthened) points. Often used for formal dress shirts.

5 *Due Bottone* Collar
The title for this collar is derived from the words for two (due) and button (bottone) in Italian. Since the collar band is tall and double buttoned, it is usually worn without a tie. This is a variation of the button-down and stand collar. Many times designers elect to use an accent color for the buttonholes and the thread used to sew on buttons.

6 Miter Collar
This collar has a miter that is like the corner of a picture frame.

Miter Collar Variations
In recent years, the stopper collar has also come to be called the miter collar. As seen in the illustration above, the most popular miter cut runs parallel to the point length.

Button-Down
Mitered collars with half-exposed buttons are also quite popular.

7 Tab Collar
A small tab is attached under the collar and fastens at the front of the neck. The tightened points spread out and make the neckline look dressy.

8 Pinhole Collar
The ends of both collar leafs are fastened with a pin by putting the pin through an eyelet that pierces the middle of the collar leaf. The necktie is then pulled over the pin. Since the pin lightly lifts the knot of the tie, this collar gives off a dressier impression than the tab collar.
Other terms: eyelet collar, pin collar.

9 Double Collar
A collar with two pieces of collar leaf on each side. Some are detachable.

10 Snap-Down Point Collar
The point is fastened with a snap to the shirt. At first glance it looks like a regular collar, but the snap-down collar bulges the points like a button-down collar.

11 Detachable Collar
Also called a false collar. Can be removed from the shirt.

12 Open Collar
General term for a collar that is not buttoned at the neck

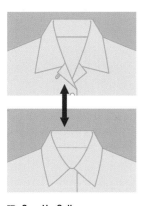

13 One-Up Collar
This is the same as the open collar, but with a button. The button can be attached either to the open collar or the shirt collar. In Japan, it is called a "Hama collar" because it became popular in the late 1970s as part of "Hamatora" (Yokohama traditional style).

14 Long-Point Collar
A collar with long points. Pointed collars create a dressy look. Antonym: short-point collar. Synonym: Barrymore collar (named after John Barrymore, a Hollywood star in 1920s, who loved wearing this particular style collar).

15 Short-Point Collar
A general term for short collars under 6 cm ($2^3/_8"$).
Synonym: tiny collar (especially for really small collars).

16 Dutch Collar
A collar with standing folds along the neckline. This type of collar is often seen in paintings by the Dutch painter Rembrandt (1606–1669). That is why it has come to be called a Dutch collar. The majority of Dutch collars are narrow and rounded.

17 Wide Spread Collar
The points are spread out wide. The angle of the point spread is approximately 100 to 130 degrees. This collar gives off a traditional European feel. Other term: Windsor collar.

18 Horizontal Collar
The points open up very wide. The angle of the points is straight like the horizon, so it is called a "horizontal" collar.

19 Round Collar
The ends of this collar are rounded, creating a soft look. Smaller rounded ends are called either round tops or round tips.

20 Wing Collar
Often seen in formal shirts, this is a standing collar with downward-folded points. Any open collar that looks like it has spreading wings may also be called a wing collar.

21 Frill Collar
Frills are attached to the neckline or the edge of the collar.

22 Jabot Collar
A collar with jabots (lace or frills attached front and center). This type of collar is seen in men's shirts primarily worn in the mid-nineteenth century, and it is used like a necktie.

23 Peter Pan Collar
A narrow and round collar. Square-shaped variations are often used in polo shirts.

24 Bow Collar
A general term for collars that are tied in a bow

Other Types of Collar

25 One-Piece Collar
A shirt collar without a band. The illustration above is called an "Italian collar." It is essentially a V-neck with a collar.

26 Stand Collar (Stand-Up Collar)
A general term for a standing collar

27 Ruffle Collar
A collar with ruffles (wide frills)

28 Sailor Collar
This is similar to the collar on a sailor's uniform. The reasons for the back collar being so large are to protect the face from strong winds on a battleship and to be able to hear orders when the collar is popped up.

29 Tie Collar
This collar gives the impression that there is actually a tie attached to a shirt or a blouse.

30 Scarf Collar
A type of oversized collar where the collar shape looks like a scarf wrapped around the neck.

31 Petal Collar
A collar cut to resemble a petal

32 Cascade Collar
"Cascade" means "waterfall" in French. The drapes attached at the base of the collar look like a waterfall.

Jacket Collar

(Tailored Collar)

A solid collar that is tailored for a man's suit. Design variations are abundant because of different styles of lapel.

1 Notched
The "notch" is where the collar ends meet the lapel. This is the general term for any collar with a notch.

2 Shawl
A type of tailored collar where it looks like the wearer has a shawl around their neck.
Other terms: roll collar, tuxedo collar.

3 Peaked Shawl Collar
A type of tailored collar. It looks like a peaked lapel but it is really a shawl collar because the V-shaped cut is in the lapel.
Other term: broad peaked lapel.

(Band Collar)

A standing collar that encircles the neck

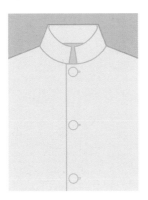

4 Cadet Collar
A collar used for cadet's uniforms

5 Chinese Collar
A type of standing collar often seen in Chinese traditional clothing.
Other term: Mandarin collar.

6 Mao Collar
A type of standing collar. The name comes from Mao Zedong, the former chairman of China. Used for Chinese national clothes. Even though the collar is folded over, this collar may be used as a synonym for the Chinese collar.
Other term: Nehru collar (named after Jawaharlal Nehru, former prime minister of India).

(Oversized Collar)

Fairly large collar

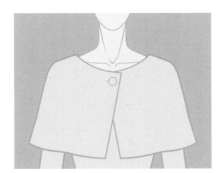

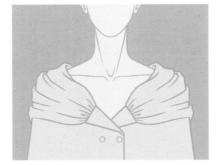

8 Fichu Collar
A type of oversized collar. The fichu is a woman's "triangular-shaped shawl" that was popular from the late eighteenth century to the early nineteenth century. The collar employs a shawl- or scarf-like shape. The neck area is exposed in a V shape, and the back is triangular. It looks as if one is wearing a scarf over the shoulders.

7 Cape Collar
A type of oversized collar. A cape-like collar.

Casual Jacket Collar

1 Dog Ear Collar
A standing collar shaped like dog's ears

2 Johnny Collar
A small shawl collar used for letterman jackets. The majority are rib-stitched.

3 Hood
A hood-shaped collar that covers the head and neck

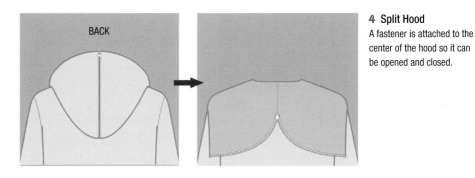

BACK

4 Split Hood
A fastener is attached to the center of the hood so it can be opened and closed.

Coat's Collar

1 Napoleonic Collar
Commonly seen in trench coats. Characterized by a turnover collar and a large lapel. It is said that the inspiration for this collar comes from Napoleonic-era military uniforms.
Other term: Bonaparte collar.

2 Ulster Collar
Usually seen on ulster coats. Both the collar and the lapel are wide and stitched. Characterized by a deep gorge (p. 68).

3 Framed Collar
As seen in Canadian coats and the trench coat. This is the general term for a collar with hemming.

Lapel

The lapel is the lower part of a tailored collar.

1 Notched Lapel
A lapel where the notch creates angles similar to a rhombus. This is the most basic type of lapel, and it is standard on single-breasted (p. 54) suits.
Other terms: step lapel, step collar.

2 Peaked Lapel
The top edges are pointy and sloped upward. This is a basic type of lapel and is standard on double-breasted (p. 55) suit jackets.
Other term: pointed lapel.

3 Seminotched Lapel
A lapel where the notch creates a more acute angle than the notched lapel

4 Semipeaked Lapel
A lapel where the notch makes a more acute angle than on a peaked lapel.
Other term: floor-level lapel.

5 L-Shaped Lapel
The collar is narrower than the lapel and the gorge line makes an L shape.

6 T-Shaped Lapel
The collar is wider than the lapel, and the gorge line makes a T shape.
Other term: inverted L shape.

7 Clover Leaf Lapel
A notched lapel where the tips of both collars and lapels are rounded. The name originates from its resemblance to a four-leaf clover.

8 Semi–Clover Leaf Lapel
This is a variation of the clover leaf lapel. Rounding either the collar or the lapel leads to a semi–clover leaf collar. Semi–clover leaf lapels are the ones with rounded lapels only.

9 Fish Mouth Lapel
A type of semi–clover leaf lapel. The name comes from its resemblance to a fish mouth.

10 Bellied Lapel
This lapel has a large curve to it.

11 Flower Lapel
The ends of the collar and the lapel are rounded. Also, the top edge of the lapel makes a shape like a flower petal.

12 Rolled Lapel
This lapel shape is often seen in traditional blazers. The lapel is rolled up enough so that it almost completely hides the buttonhole of the first button.

Body Front

Shirts

Bosom The chest area of a shirt

1 Frilled Bosom
The front center of the shirt is frilled.

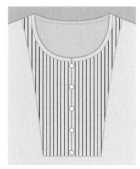

2 Pleated Bosom
Vertically pleated from bust to hem. Pleats can be added by sewing on a dickey.

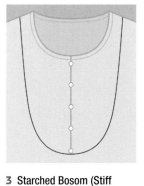

3 Starched Bosom (Stiff Bosom)
A chest fitting that is U shaped or square shaped and starched stiff

4 Gather
Wrinkles and pleats made by sewing fabric down while making soft folds

Placket (Placket Front)

The opening of a garment

1 Placket Front
The placket is folded over the front. A narrow band of box pleats are sewn on the placket.
Other terms: panel front, top center box pleats, British front.

2 French Front
The placket is folded back (inside the shirt).
Other term: no-front placket.

3 Fly Front
The fly front covers up the buttons. Other term: covered placket.

4 Half Placket
At a glance this placket looks like a pullover.

5 Pullover
The placket doesn't continue to the hem.

6 Teardrop Placket
A teardrop-shaped placket

7 Lace-Up Front
The placket is fastened with a string.

Jacket

Front Cut

The curve on a jacket's lower edge

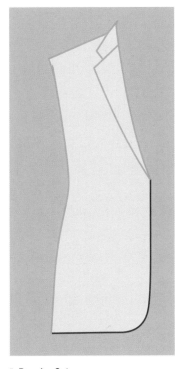

1 Regular Cut

The lower edge of the jacket is rounded. This cut is regularly seen in single-breasted suit jackets.

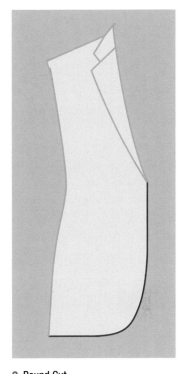

2 Round Cut

The lower edge of a jacket is even more rounded than the regular cut.

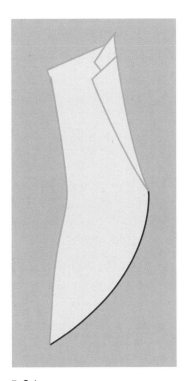

3 Cutaway

The lower edge of the jacket is rounded diagonally around the hips.

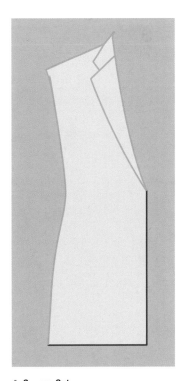

4 Square Cut

Often seen in double-breasted jackets. The lower edge of the jacket is cut square.

The Relationship between the Center of a Jacket and Its Buttons
Single Breasted = SB

This is a jacket that has one column of buttons up the
center. From here on, single breasted will be abbreviated as
SB for convenience.

1 SB One-Button Jacket (S One-Button)

2 SB Two-Button Jacket (S Two-Button): the top button is done up (low-button stance).

3 SB Two-Button Jacket (S Two-Button): both buttons are done up (high-button stance).

4 SB Three-Button Jacket (S Three-Button): the top two buttons are done up.

5 SB Three-Button Jacket (S Three-Button): the middle button is done up.

6 3-Roll-2 ($^3/_2$ roll): rolled lapel

The Relationship between the Center of a Jacket and Its Buttons
Double Breasted = DB

The center of this jacket has a deep overlap and two columns of buttons. Hereafter, double breasted is abbreviated as DB for convenience.

7 Four-on-One: fasten one button out of four.
The button stance is spread out across the right and left sides.

8 Four-on-Two: fasten two buttons out of four.
Both sides have the same button stance.

9 Six-on-One: fasten one button out of six.

10 Six-on-Two: fasten two buttons out of six.

11 Six-on-Three: fasten three buttons out of six.

Shoulder

Shoulder line   The line of a garment created for the shoulders

1 Shirt Shoulder
A shoulder line without shoulder pads, like a shirt

2 Rounded Shoulder
A shoulder line that has an overall roundness to it

3 Natural Shoulder
This is a naturally rounded shoulder line that uses very little or no shoulder padding. Often used for Ivy League–style blazers.

4 British Natural Shoulder
The natural shoulder line in traditional British jackets. This shoulder line tends to fall somewhere between a natural shoulder and concave shoulder.

5 Concave Shoulder
A shoulder line that arches from the base of the neck to the shoulder, like an upside-down bow.

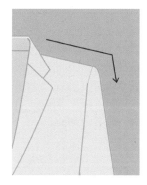

6 Square Shoulder
The shoulder looks squared off and slightly lifted. Looks straighter than a natural shoulder line.

7 Block Shoulder
This is a squared shoulder line, as if a block were inserted under the shoulder line. It is broader and thicker than the square shoulder line.

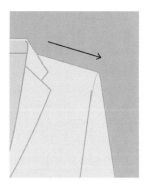

8 Straight Shoulder
A shoulder line that is straightened out

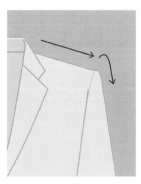

9 Built-Up Shoulder
A shoulder line that is extended and has a raised sleeve head. Other term: roped shoulder.

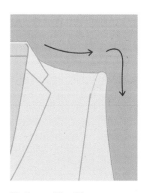

10 Power Shoulder
The sleeve head is quite raised, thus creating a powerful shoulder line.

11 Big Shoulder
A shoulder line with a broad shoulder width.
Other terms: broad shoulder.
Antonym: narrow shoulder.

12 Wing Shoulder
A shoulder line that has a winglike extension

Armhole   General term for a sleeve hole

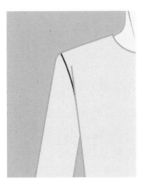

1 Set-In Sleeve
This is the most natural way of attaching a sleeve. It is used for well-made, tailored jackets and coats. When garments with these sleeves are placed on the ground, the sleeve sits down.
Other term: normal sleeve.

2 Shirt Sleeve
A straight-line sleeve used for ordinary shirts. When garments with these sleeves are naturally placed on the ground, they create the shape of a capital "T."

3 Raglan Sleeve
This sleeve has a seam from the underarm to the collarbone. The shoulder and sleeve make a single piece. Lord Raglan of Britain invented the Raglan sleeve during the Crimean War (1853–1856). The Raglan sleeve has excellent functionality and made it easy for wounded soldiers to change their clothes. The Raglan sleeve is also used for trench coats (p. 20).

4 Semi-Raglan Sleeve
The armhole seam curves toward the neck approximately halfway to the top of the shoulder.

5 Epaulet Sleeve
The armhole seam makes it appear as though an epaulet were attached.

6 Wedge Sleeve
An armhole seam that makes a wedge shape

7 Dropped Shoulder
A shoulder line where the sleeve head is lower than the regular armhole seam. Often seen in shirts and sweaters.

8 Kimono Sleeve
A sleeve that is cut in with the bodice, similar to a kimono

9 French Sleeve
In Europe and America, the French sleeve is treated as a synonym for the kimono sleeve. However, in Japan, the French sleeve refers to a sleeve that is very short.
Other term: Chinese sleeve.

10 American Sleeve
Here there is actually no sleeve. Also, the cut is deeply curved from the base of the neck to the underarm.

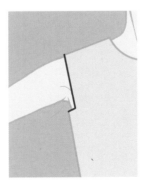

11 Square Armhole
Sleeveless with a squared armhole

Sleeves

Sleeves

Sleeves are an extremely significant element, as far as design and functionality are concerned, because they greatly affect the silhouette of the garment.

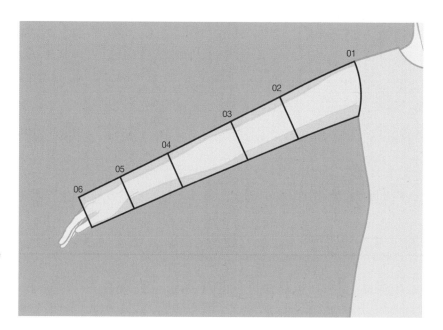

1 Sleeve Length
01 Sleeveless (tank): No sleeve
02 Short sleeve: T-shirt sleeve
03 Elbow length: A sleeve that ends at the elbow
04 Three-quarter length: A sleeve that covers ¾ of the arm. Also known as a bracelet.
05 Long: A sleeve that ends at the wrist
06 Extra long: Long enough to cover the hand. Some have a thumbhole.

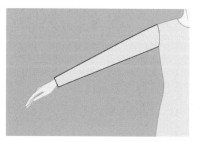

2 Fitted Sleeve
A narrow sleeve

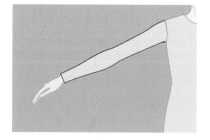

3 Sheath Sleeve
A sheathlike, long, narrow sleeve

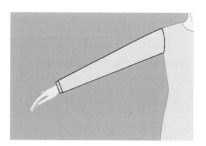

4 Telescope Sleeve
A type of doubled sleeve reminiscent of the cylinder of a telescope

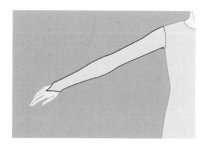

5 Fitted Point Sleeve
Often seen in wedding gowns. A sleeve that extends to the back of the hand. Shaped like a sharp "V."

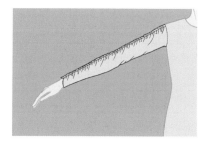

6 Mousquetaire Sleeve
A long and narrow sleeve with shirring over the vertical seam

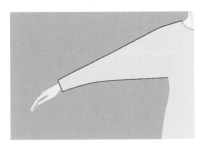

7 Dolman Sleeve
A long sleeve that is wide at the armhole and gently narrows toward the wrist

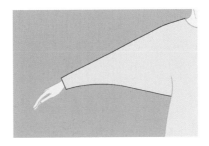

8 Batwing Sleeve
A sleeve shaped like the wings of a bat. Other term: Magyar sleeve.

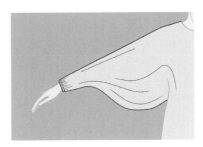

9 Bag Sleeve
A sleeve that sags

10 Bell Sleeve
A sleeve that flares out like a bell. Synonyms: trumpet sleeve, cornet sleeve, Mandarin sleeve.

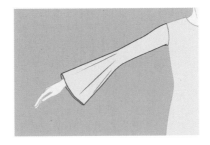

11 Pagoda Sleeve
A type of bell sleeve. The sleeve is flared toward the hem like a pagoda. There is also a tiered variation.

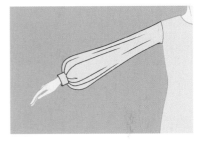

12 Bishop Sleeve
This sleeve is characterized by the shape often seen in a priest's garb where the section below the elbow is bigger and fuller. Other term: peasant sleeve.

13 Chicken Leg Sleeve
A sleeve shaped like a chicken's leg. The sleeve head has volume and then narrows toward the cuff.

14 Leg-of-Mutton Sleeve
A sleeve shaped like a leg of mutton

15 Juliet Sleeve
A long, narrow sleeve that is attached to a puffed upper sleeve. This sleeve originated with Shakespeare's Romeo and Juliet.

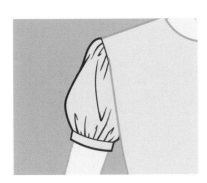

16 Puffed Sleeve
An inflated sleeve that forms a round shape by using gathers and tucks

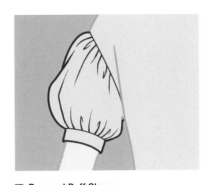

17 Dropped Puff Sleeve
A puffed sleeve with the armhole seam located lower than the shoulder

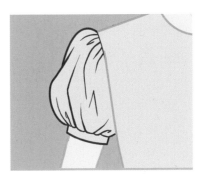

18 Balloon Sleeve
A large and puffy sleeve like a balloon. Puffier than the puff sleeve.

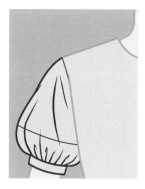

19 Lantern Sleeve
A round sleeve made using darts and seams

20 Tiered Sleeve
A layered sleeve made using design seams

21 Cape Sleeve
A sleeve that gently flares out from the shoulder to the cuff, as if one were wearing a cape

22 Caplet Sleeve
Similar to the cape sleeve but shorter

23 Circular Sleeve
A type of cape sleeve. It flares out like the wings of a bird.
Other terms: angel sleeve (originated with angels frequently seen in paintings).

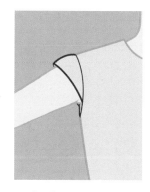

24 Cap Sleeve
A short sleeve that looks like a cap on the shoulder

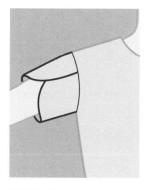

25 Petal Sleeve
A sleeve that looks like a flower petal.
Synonym: tulip sleeve.

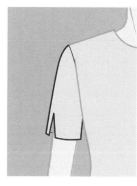

26 Slash Sleeve
A sleeve that has a small slit

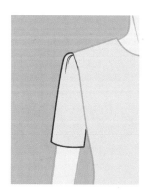

27 Tucked Sleeve
A sleeve with a tucked sleeve cap

28 Roll-Up Sleeve
A sleeve that can be rolled up. To prevent the fold from coming undone, some of these sleeves have buttons.

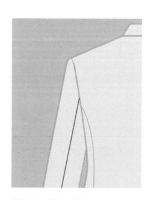

29 Two-Piece Sleeve
Two pieces of fabric that are put together to make a sleeve. Usually seen in well-made, tailored jackets and coats.

Cuff(s)   General term for the band-like fabric attached at the lower edge of a sleeve

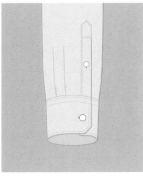

Round-Cut Cuff

Angled-Cut Cuff

1 Single Cuff
Not double folded

2 Double Cuff
Double-folded cuffs fasten with cuff links.
Other terms: French cuff, link cuff.

3 Adjustable Cuff
The cuff size can be adjusted.

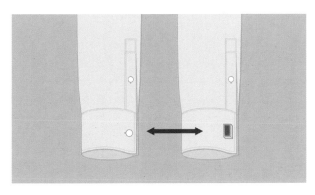

4 Convertible Cuff
A single cuff that can be fastened with a cuff link

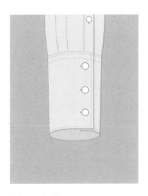

5 Long Cuff
A cuff with an overly thick cuff width

6 Button Cuff
A cuff fastened with a decorative button

7 Straight Cuff
Connected straight from the sleeve to the cuff

8 Turn-Up
General term for a folded cuff. This is a type of double cuff.

9 Open Cuff
There is an opening, such as a slit, on the cuff.

10 Removable Cuff
A cuff that can be fastened or undone using buttons. By contrast, a cuff with nonfunctional buttons is called an imitation cuff.
Other term: surgeon's cuff.

11 Winged Cuff

A cuff that is shaped like the wings of a bird.
Other term: pointed cuff.

12 Gauntlet Cuff

A cuff that resembles the armored gloves used by medieval knights

13 Bell-Shaped Cuff

A cuff shaped like a bell.
Other term: dropped cuff.

14 Circular Cuff

The fabric of this cuff is cut in a circular shape, and a flare is then added.
Other terms: wind cuff, ruffle cuff.

15 Extension Cuff

In this case, extension means "to spread." Therefore this is a cuff that flares out or spreads.

16 Piping Cuff

A thin piping-like cuff

17 Ribbon Cuff

A ribbonlike cuff that allows the wrist size to be adjusted

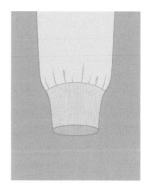

18 Knitted Cuff

A rib-stitched cuff. Often seen in casual jackets.

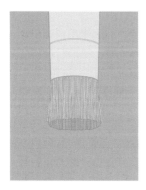

19 Fringed Cuff

Fringes (p. 69) are attached around this cuff.

20 Zipped Cuff

A zipper is attached to this type of cuff.

Body Rear

Shirts and Blouses: Body Rear

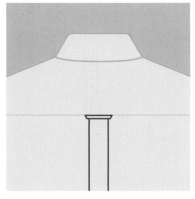

1 Back Center Boxed Pleat
A box pleat is added to the center of the back on this shirt. The loop above the pleat is for hanging the shirt.

2 Side Pleat
Pleats are added on the sides of the shirt back.

3 Side Tuck
Tucks are added on the sides of the shirt back.

4 Split Shoulder Yoke
The shoulder yoke is split in half.

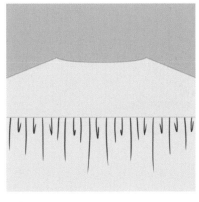

5 Gather
The use of abundant wrinkles and pleats brings about a certain softness.

6 Teardrop Back
There is a teardrop-shaped opening on the back.

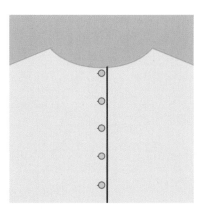

7 Full Open
The back can be fully opened.

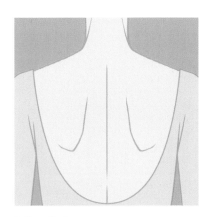

8 Bare Back
The back is exposed.

Backs of Suit Jackets

Vent (Vents)

A slit in the back of a suit jacket or a coat. Vents were created in order to allow the jacket to be more flexible while riding a horse. The edges of the vents overlap.

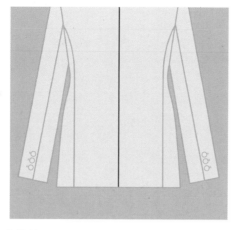

1 No Vent
A particular design that doesn't have a vent.
Other term: without vent.

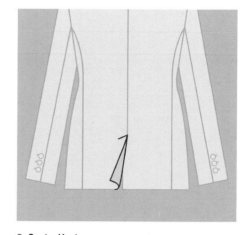

2 Center Vent
The vent is at the center of the back seam (p. 69).

Other Types of Slits

Slits: Vertical gaps or a cut in the bottom of a garment. Rather than serving a simple decorative purpose, slits actually increase functionality and allow for easier movement. The openings do not overlap.
Slash: A type of slit. A slash is for more decorative purposes. Slashes do not necessarily run lengthwise; some slashes have curves.

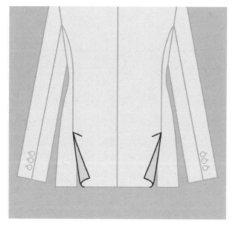

3 Side Vents
There is a vent on each side seam.

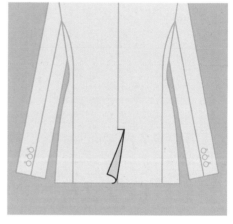

4 Hook Vent (Center Hook Vent)
A hooklike center vent

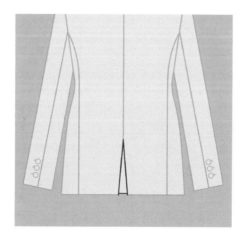

5 Inverted Vent
This is a vent that increases the garment's ease of movement. It uses an inverted pleat (p. 71).

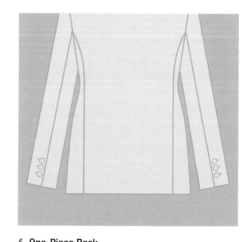

6 One-Piece Back
Since the back of the jacket is tailored from a single piece of fabric, there is no back seam. If you are adding a vent, it is going to be only a shallow side vent.

Hemline

The lower edge of a garment

Variations on Tops: Hemline

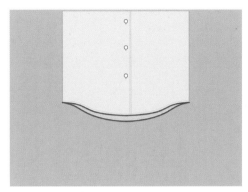

1 Tail Bottom
In the old days, shirts were worn as underwear. Instead of wearing briefs, the tail of a shirt was tucked in to cover the crotch. The so-called "tail bottom" is a remnant of this practice. Other term: tail shirt.

2 Square Bottom
The hem of the shirt is straight, causing the bottom edge to make a square silhouette. When the hem at the bottom of a shirt is straight, it is called a square hem.

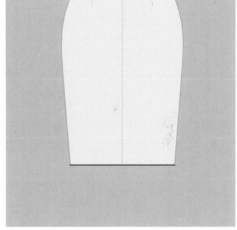

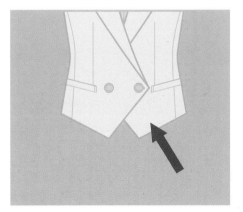

3 Pointed Front
A hem that makes a triangular shape. Other term: waistcoat hem.

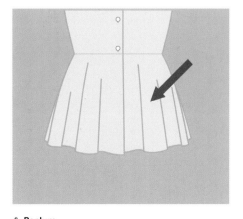

4 Peplum
Peplum is the flared portion below the waistline. The waistline is shapely, and the hem has volumes that emphasize femininity.

Variations on Bottoms: Hemline

FRONT

5 Flamenco Hem
A type of layered hem (p. 66). The front hemline is shorter, while the back is longer. This hemline is reminiscent of Spanish flamenco dance attire.

6

Single Cuff
This is a type of cuff where the hem of pants is not rolled up.

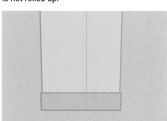

Turn-Up
The hem is turned up and pressed. The fold line is solid.
Other terms: double cuff, cuffed bottom.

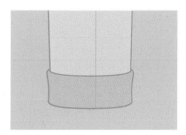

Roll-Up
The hem is rolled.

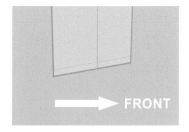

FRONT

Morning Cut
The hem is angled so that the pants are shorter in the front and longer at the back. Usually the difference in elevation is approximately 1.5 to 2 cm ($^5/_8$″ to $^6/_8$″).

Other Hemline Variations

7 Flare
This hemline flares toward the bottom and gives off a soft and wavy impression.

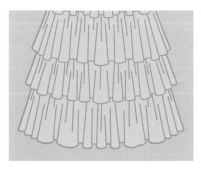

8 Tiered
Layered frills of varying lengths that overlap create a tiered look.

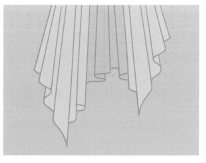

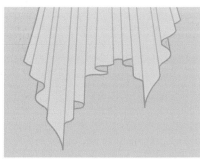

9 Irregular Hemline
This is simply an uneven hemline.
Other terms: handkerchief hemline, uneven hemline.

Details

General term for any detailed designs within a garment

Details for Tops and Bottoms

1 Shirring
Wavy pleats created by sewing down appropriately spaced gathers

2 Drapes
Soft folds and curves created when fabric hangs down. Drapes give the impression of elegance.

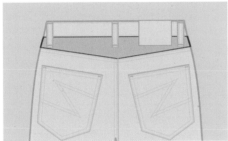

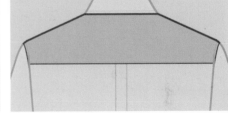

3 Yoke
A piece of fabric fitted to a garment for the purpose of reinforcement or as a design element

---

Fastener

A device that allows fastening and unfastening with the simple up-and-down movement of a metal fitting.
Other terms: zipper (zip), fly.

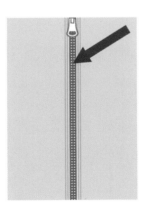

4 Exposed Zipper
A zipper with an exposed chain. The chain is where a zipper's teeth meet.

5 Covered Zipper
A zipper with a hidden chain. Hiding the chain prevents it from directly touching bare skin.

6 Head-to-Head Zipper
A zipper that can fasten and unfasten from either end.
Other term: coverall zipper.

Tops: Details

Shirts: Details

1 Collar Band

The band portion of any shirt collar.
Other terms: collar stand, collar base.

2 Collar Leaf

The part of the collar that is attached to the
collar band. May simply be called "the collar."
Other term: top collar.

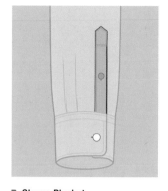

3 Sleeve Placket

A narrow piece of fabric attached to
the vertical opening of a sleeve

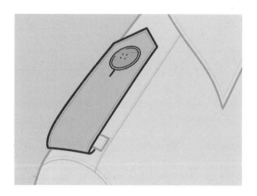

4 Epaulet

A tab-shaped piece of fabric on the shoulder of a garment.
Epaulets on trench coats serve the function of a fastener to
carry a gun or binoculars.
Other term: shoulder loop.

5 Cuff Links

A general term for any decorative
button attached to the cuff.
Other term: cuff buttons.

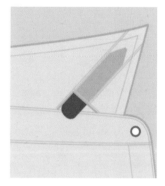

6 Collar Stays

These pieces of plastic are inserted
from the underside of the collar as a
stabilizing tool.
Other terms: collar sticks, bones.

Jackets: Details

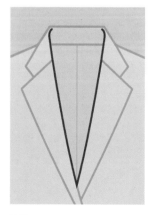

7 V-zone

A V-shaped line formed by the roll
line of a jacket

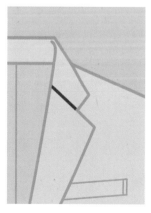

8 Gorge

Where the collar and lapels meet

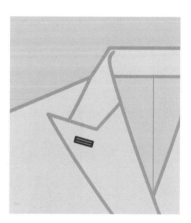

9 Lapel Hole

A buttonhole on a lapel

10 Trimming
This is a piece of fabric, such as bias tape, wrapped around the edges of a garment and used for antifray or decorative purposes. Other term: piping.

11 Coat of Arms
A shield-shaped crest used by nobles in Europe to symbolize family lineage. Today, the coat of arms is used for blazer badges to show the name of one's school or sports club.
Other terms: crest, blazer badge.

12 Elbow Patch
Leather or fabric patches for the elbow

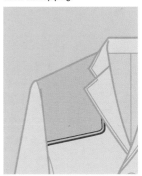

13 Gun Patch
A patch of fabric used to support the butt of a gun

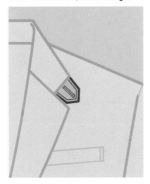

14 Throat Tab
A tab attached to the edge of a tailored collar. The tab is buttoned to make the collar stand up, and since it is located next to the throat, it is called a throat tab.
Other term: throat latch.

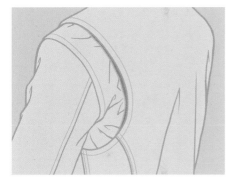

15 Action Pleat
This is a pleat at the back. The pleat increases ease of movement.

16 Fringe
Also known as a tassel. It is a frayed fabric edge. Used for scarves, shawls, western jackets, etc.

17 Back Seam
Center seam on the back of a garment

18 Buckle
A fastening device used for belts or shoes

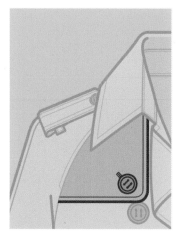

19 Storm Flap

A patch that is attached on the shoulder to prevent rain from entering during extreme weather. Often seen on trench coats. It can also serve as a gun patch, because trench coats are actually army uniforms.
Other term: storm patch.

20 Caped Back

Cape-shaped back yoke. Two pieces of fabric are layered on the back, where rain is most likely to enter a garment, in order to increase rain proofing. In total, there are three layers, including the actual back, so it is very sturdy.

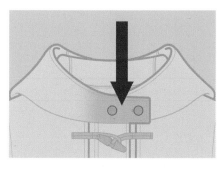

21 Chin Warmer

A piece of fabric used to warm the chin. The chin warmer also keeps wind and rain from blowing in through the collar.
Other terms: chinstrap, chin flap.

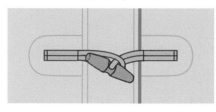

22 Toggle

Wooden or metal buttons shaped like floating rings. Used for duffle coats.

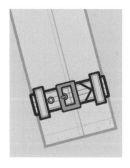

23 Cuff Strap

A belt on the cuff that can be fastened to prevent wind from blowing up a sleeve

24 Loop Buttonhole

A ring-shaped buttonhole

25 Back Belt

A belt attached to the back of the waist. Some are not detachable because they are sewn directly to the fabric.

26 Drawstring

A string used to adjust the size of an opening

27 How to wear the hood of a parka

① When worn properly, the hood covers the neck and head entirely. The back of the hood is either squared off or rounded.

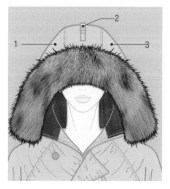

② A hood with depth is usually divided into three panels.

③ Often, the hood is down. When down, it is folded and exposes the inside of the hood.

Bottoms: Details

Design Variation for Pleats

A pleat is created in order to increase ease of movement and to bring out the three-dimensional feel of a garment. Unlike tucks, the folded line doesn't disappear in the middle. It stays folded all the way to the bottom. Pleats are used at the front and back of a bodice or skirt.

1 Knife Pleats
Pleats folded in a single direction. Other term: side pleats.

2 Box Pleats
Box-shaped pleats where the folds meet under the garment

3 Inverted Pleats
Inverted box pleats are box pleats where the fold is reversed.

4 Accordion Pleats
Pleats folded narrowly, so that they are shaped like the bellows of an accordion

5 Umbrella Pleats
Pleats that are folded flaring toward the hem like an umbrella

6 Crystal Pleats
Pleats where the folded line stands out like a crystal. The width of the pleat is fairly narrow, ranging from 2 to 4 mm (approximately ⅛″).

7 Curved Pleats
Take even narrower pleats at upper part of accordion pleats and curve the folds. If curved pleats is added to bottom of a skirt, the curve beautifully follow a body line.

8 Fancy Pleats
These pleats are "whimsical." The illustration above shows folds that are alternating left to right.

9 Random Pleats
Pleats are folded in random widths.

10 Fortuny Pleats
A type of random pleat. These pleats flow beautifully, by using plenty of fabric, and make a creative wave. Invented by Spanish designer Mariano Fortuny, who used ideas from ancient Grecian dresses.

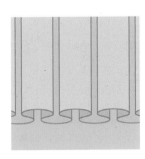

11 Unpressed Pleats
Soft pleats without solid folds. Other terms: soft pleats. Synonym: cartridge pleats (shaped like cartridges, narrow tube-shaped pleats).

Other Types of Details

1 Gore
Triangle-shaped, small pieces of fabric

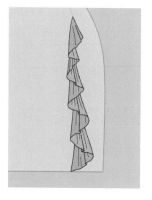

2 Cascade
A cascade is a small waterfall. This is a decorative fabric piece that looks like water running down from a waterfall.

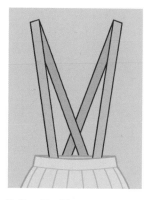

3 Shoulder Straps
Straps that hang over the shoulder

4 Side Tabs
A tab for adjusting the size of the waist. Often used on pants without belt loops and hems on a jacket.

5 Trouser Braid
Decorative tape on both sides of the pants. Other term: tuxedo stripe.

6 Hammer Loop
A loop-like band attached to the side of a pair of pants for carrying a hammer

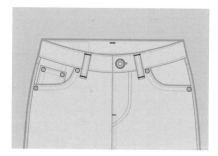

7 Bar Tack
An end stitch for fasteners and pocket openings. Performed for reinforcing purposes.

8 Rivet
Formerly called a copper rivet. Copper rivets were attached for reinforcement to prevent end stitches on fasteners and pocket openings from coming apart. Often used instead of a bar tack.

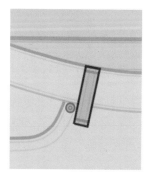

9 Belt Loop
A loop for holding a belt in place

10 Leather Patch
A leather patch attached on the rear right side of the waist belt on a pair of jeans. Information such as the brand name, product name, lot number, and size is listed on the patch.

Pockets
Pocket outside a garment: outside pocket
Pocket inside a garment: inside pocket

Design Variations for the Pocket on Tops

Chest pocket
Attached on either one side or both
Other term: breast pocket

1 Square Pocket
A square-shaped outside pocket on a shirt

2 Round Pocket
A rounded-corner, outside pocket on a shirt

3 Pentagon Pocket
A pentagon-shaped, outside pocket on a shirt

Side Pocket
A pocket located beside the hip.
Other term: waist pocket.

4 Button-Up Pocket
Most often seen in shirts, this is a pentagon-shaped outside pocket where the opening fastens with a button.

5 Button Flap Pocket
An outside pocket with a flap that is fastened with a button

6 Crescent Pocket
A crescent-shaped, inside pocket

7 Welt Pocket
A type of inside pocket often seen on a jacket.
Other terms: box pocket, slit pocket.

1 Piped Pocket
General term for pockets that have a piped style
① Single-piped pocket ② Double-piped pocket

2 Flap Pocket
A pocket with a flap

3 Patch Pocket
A pocket applied on the outside of a garment.
Other terms: out pocket, set-in pocket.

4 Patch-and-Flap Pocket
A patch pocket with a flap

5 Pleated Pocket
The center of a patch pocket is pleated, thus increasing the pocket's capacity.

6 Scalloped Pocket
Scalloped refers to the shape of "scallop shell." An upside-down mountain shape.

7 Framed Patch Pocket
The flap is applied on a patch pocket so that it appears to be piped.

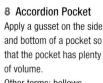

8 Accordion Pocket
Apply a gusset on the side and bottom of a pocket so that the pocket has plenty of volume.
Other terms: bellows pocket, gusset pocket.

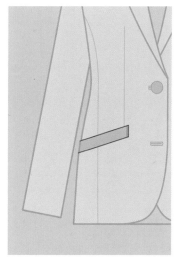

9 Slanted Pocket
A pocket applied at an angle.
Other terms: hacking pocket, angled pocket.

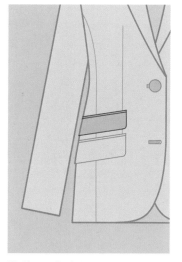

10 Change Pocket
A small, flapped coin pocket located above the side pocket of a jacket

Other Types of Pockets

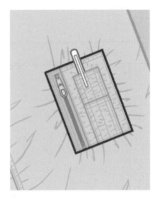

1 Muff Pocket

A pocket that opens vertically in order allow one to warm their hands.
Other term: hand warmer.
① Parka's muff pocket ② Peacoat's muff pockets

2 Kangaroo Pocket

A large pocket that covers everything from the chest to the stomach.
Other term: center pocket.

3 Pen Pocket

A pen pocket is attached to the left arm of army uniforms such as the MA-1 and N3-B. Its distinctive features are a small fastened pocket and a pen holder with a plastic device inserted to prevent the tip of a pen from piercing the bottom of the pocket.

Design Variation of Pockets Found on Pants

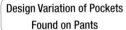

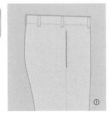 

1 Slash Pocket

A pocket applied utilizing the vertical seam of a garment.
① Seam pocket: Applied using the seam of a garment.
Other term: vertical pocket.
② Forward-set pocket: A pocket applied at an angle.
Other term: slanted pocket.

2 L-pocket

The slit of this pocket makes an L shape.

3 Riveted Jeans Pocket

The standard pocket applied to jeans. Both ends of an L-pocket are reinforced with a rivet (p. 72). Other terms: western pocket, frontier pocket.

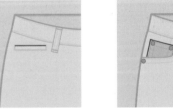

4 Crescent-Shaped Pocket

A pocket shaped like a crescent

5 Horizontal Pocket

The slit is cut horizontally.
Other term: horizontal slit.

6 Fob Pocket

A "fob" is a small pocket for storing a watch. Some have a flap.
Other terms: watch pocket, watch fob pocket.

7 Coin Pocket

A type of fob pocket. Often applied on jeans, it is a small coin pocket.

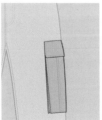

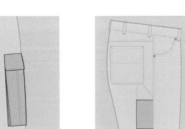

8 Cargo Pocket

A pocket applied to both sided of a pair of cargo pants. Many of them have gussets.

9 Tool Pocket

Often applied to painter pants, this is a vertically elongated pocket for holding tools.

10 Hip Pocket
A general term for a pocket on the hips

① **Button-Through Pocket**
Buttoned-down piped pocket

② **Flap and Button-Down Pocket**
Other term: pistol pocket (originally for carrying for a small pistol)

③ **Frog Pocket**
The button is fastened with a loop stitched over the pocket.

Stitches

A stitch is simply "the method by which a piece of thread is used to sew fabric."

1 Single Stitch
Straight-line single stitch. Other term: straight stitch.

2 Double Stitch
Two lines of stitches that are parallel. Used primarily for reinforcement.

3 Stitched Edge
A stitch applied along the edge and the seam of a garment for the purposes of reinforcement and design.

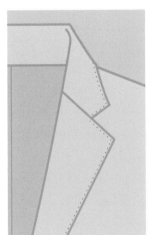

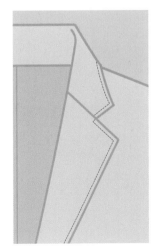

4 Blind Stitch
A subtle starlike stitch

5 Saddle Stitch
This is a single stitch, sewn from both the front and the back, with a single piece of thread that is threaded through two needles (one on each end of the thread). Compared to sewing-machine stitches, the saddle stitch is highly labor intensive. However, this seam won't loosen, because if one side ever becomes loose, the other side will hold the seam tight.

Section 3 Design Variations for Accessories

Footwear   Different types of shoes

Footwear Variations

The name of the shoe changes based on the position and design of the mouth.

1 Pumps
The instep is exposed.

2 Shoe
The mouth is located below the ankle.

3 Sneaker
Sport shoes

4 Booties
A type of woman's ankle boot

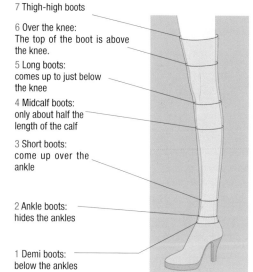

7 Thigh-high boots

6 Over the knee:
The top of the boot is above the knee.

5 Long boots:
comes up to just below the knee

4 Midcalf boots:
only about half the length of the calf

3 Short boots:
come up over the ankle

2 Ankle boots:
hides the ankles

1 Demi boots:
below the ankles

6 Boots Sandal
Boots with open toes like sandals

5 Boots
The mouth of these shoes comes up over the ankle. Boots have different names depending on their length.

7 Sandal
Slip-on footwear that doesn't cover the entire foot

8 Slipper
Sandals that are worn inside

Design Variations on Shoe Mouths

The position and design of the shoe mouth determine the name of the shoe.

1 Blucher
A style where the quarter is over the vamp

2 Balmoral
A style where the quarter is sewn inside the vamp

3 Monk Strap
A buckle is attached to the vamp. Invented by Alpine monks in the fifteenth century.

4 Fastener
Simply pulling down on a fastener allows the mouth of the shoe to open, so fasteners are often found on boots. The position of the fastener doesn't necessarily matter. It can be on the front, the inside, or the outside of the boot. The illustration above shows an outside zipper.

5 Side Gore
An elastic gore applied to the side of a shoe

6 Button-Up
Button-ups are located on the outside of the boot. Some are actually zippers, instead of buttons, and occasionally nonfunctional buttons are attached as a decoration.

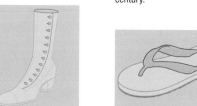

7 Thong
Sandals with straps

Details Major elements that make up shoes are summarized here.

1 Oxford Shoes

The mouth is a lace-up. The illustration below shows a Brogues Oxford shoe.
Other terms: wingtip shoes (winglike, W shaped, decorative stitching).

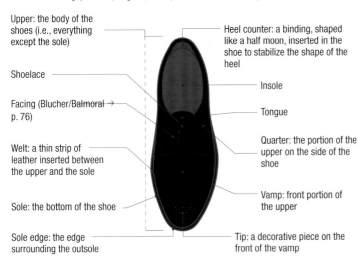

Upper: the body of the shoes (i.e., everything except the sole)

Heel counter: a binding, shaped like a half moon, inserted in the shoe to stabilize the shape of the heel

Shoelace

Facing (Blucher/Balmoral → p. 76)

Insole

Tongue

Quarter: the portion of the upper on the side of the shoe

Welt: a thin strip of leather inserted between the upper and the sole

Vamp: front portion of the upper

Sole: the bottom of the shoe

Sole edge: the edge surrounding the outsole

Tip: a decorative piece on the front of the vamp

3 Converse All Star

A sneaker by Converse. Canvas or leather uppers with a rubber sole. There are two types: HI-cut, where the upper covers the ankle, and OX-cut, where the ankle is exposed. The illustration shows an OX-cut. These shoes are quite simple and perfectly designed to easily match any type of clothing.

Tongue

Shoelace

Upper

Insole

Eyelet

Toe cap (tip, design on the toe)

2 Doc Martens

Doc Martens is a German shoemaker. Eight-Hole Boots, shown in the illustration below, were loved by the British working class. In the late 1960s, these boots became quite popular among skinheads and then hit the punk scene in the 1970s. As a result, the boots have become a must-have for many youths.

Shoelace

Finger pull loop

Boot shaft

Back stay

Vamp

Heel counter

Shank (arch of the foot)

Outsole: The portion of the sole that touches the ground. In the illustration, we see a "bouncing sole." This is an air-cushioned sole invented by Doc Martens from Germany.

4 High-Heel Pumps

Designed for women to bring out femininity by making the legs appear elongated

Vamp

Heel

Heel cap (can be changed out when worn down)

Toe

Outsole

Design Variation for the Sole and Heel

The sole is the bottom of the shoes. The heel is only the back.

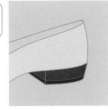

1 Low Heel
Below 3 cm (1⅛") in height

2 Middle Heel
3 to 5 cm (1⅛" to 2") in height

3 High Heel
Above 7 cm (2¾") in height

4 Pin Heel
A heel that is narrow like a needle

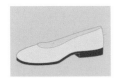

5 Flat Heel
A type of low heel. 1 cm to 2 cm (1⅛" to 1¾") in height, with a wide heel.

6 Pinafore Heel
A flat heel that connects the heel to the toe

7 Wedge Sole
High at the heel and becoming low toward the toe

8 Platform Sole
Both the toe and heel are high.

9 Hidden Heel
At first glance it looks like a flat heel, but in reality a hidden heels makes the wearer appear taller.

Design Variations for the Toe

1 Plain Toe
The most common type of toe. No design.

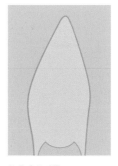

2 Pointed Toe
The toe is more pointed than normal.
Other terms: Italian cut, winkle pickers, needle toe.

3 Square Toe
The toe is squared off.

4 Round Square Toe
Corners of the square toe are rounded.
Other term: plant toe.

5 Round Toe
The toe is more rounded than usual.

6 Oblique Toe
The toe is cut at an angle.

7 Balloon Toe
The toe is round and puffy like a balloon.
Other terms: bubble toe, forehead toe.

8 Open Toe
The toes peek out from inside the shoe.

Tip — A decorative leather piece over the toes. The front, designed portion of the vamp.

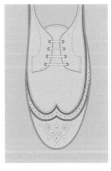

1 Wing Tip
A W-shaped piece of material on the vamp, in the shape of wings, with decorative stitching

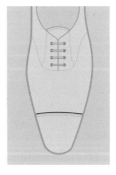

2 Straight Tip
A straight line of stitching that cuts horizontally across the vamp

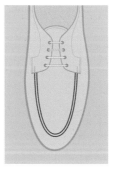

3 U-tip
U-shaped stitches on the vamp

4 Toe Cap
A design piece attached to the toe

Straps — A belt-like fastening piece for securing the shoe to the foot

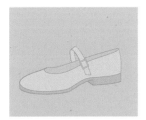

1 One-Strap Shoes
A single strap attached to the instep of the shoe

2 T-strap Shoes
T-shaped straps are used.

3 Cross-Strap
Straps that cross at the instep

4 Ankle Strap
A strap that fastens high up on the ankle

Other Details

1 Boot Seams

There are variations on how the shaft and the uppers (the portion that encloses the foot) are seamed.

① The quarter and the boot shaft are seamed together.

② The vamp and the heel counter are seamed together.

③ The upper is one piece and seamed together with the shaft.

2 Metal Eyelet
An eyelet made from any type of metal

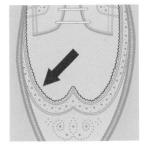

3 Pinking
V-shaped zigzag stitches on the vamp

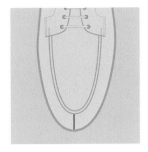

4 Center Seam
The vertical stitch on the toe of the shoe

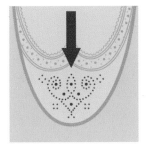

5 Medallion
Small punched design on the toe. Other term: perforation.

Headwear   Any item worn on the head, such as a hat

Hat   A type of hat where the brim encircles the crown. The illustration below shows a soft hat.

Center crease — Tip
Pinch
Side crown
Crown
Brim
Shoulder (where the crown and the brim meet)
Hatband
Underbrim (underside of the brim)
Edge (edge of the brim)

Cap   A hat without a brim OR a hat that has a brim only at the front. The illustration is an example of a baseball cap.

Crown
Top button: Fastens the entire cap together.
Eyelet: vent hole
Peak
Sandwich
LOVE.
Meshed material is used for some caps in order to make them breathable. The illustration is an example of a "back mesh." It uses nylon mesh behind the crown.
Some caps have an adjustable closure.

Sweatband: A band attached inside of a cap that guarantees a snug fit. Usually made out of a fabric other than leather. The sweatband directly touches the head, so materials with softness, sweat absorbency, and dryness are the most sought after.

Accessories

Ornaments and decorations

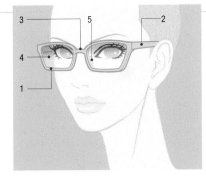

1 Eyeglasses

The four key points for designing regular glasses and sunglasses are listed.

1 Rims: Frames around the lenses. This is the most important element of the glasses. Rims dictate the overall impression of the glasses.
2 Temple: the portion on the side of the face
3 Bridge: a part that connects two lenses
4 Lens: Just adding a little color or gradation can truly transform the look of any pair of glasses.
5 Nose pad

2 Hair Accessory
Headband, tiara, headdress, etc.

3 Earrings
There are clip-on style or screw-on style.

4 Pierced Earrings
An earring that is worn in a hole pierced through the ears

5 Necklace
There are different styles: chain, pendant, beads, and more.

6 Choker
A necklace worn tightly around the neck

7 Necktie
A band or string-shaped accessory worn around the neck. Usually matches the shirt.

8 Brooch
An accessory used to fasten a scarf or a tie to the shirt. Can also be a simple ornament worn on the chest. Items in this category include corsages, cameos (an ornamental carving on a gem or a seashell), and more.

9 Bracelet
An ornament worn around the wrist. In a broader sense, a watch can actually be a bracelet.

10 Ring
Designs and prices vary greatly depending on whether gems, glass, beads, or precious metals are used.

11 Gloves
There are two types: gloves, where the fingers are separated, or mittens, where only the thumb is separated.

12 Nail Art
Decorations and art on the nails. Manicures, artificial fingernails, and more.

13 Armlet
A ring worn on the upper arm. Bangles, scrunchies (originally used to tie the hair up), etc.

14 Anklet
A ring worn around the ankle

15 Toe Ring
A ring worn on the toes

16 Pedicure
A type of nail art painted onto the toenails

17 Cloth
Worn around the neck and shoulders for coordination. How the cloth is worn depends on its size and purpose.
Handkerchief: A square-shaped piece of fabric used for wiping the hands or mouth. Materials used for handkerchiefs include cotton, silk, linen, and others.
Bandanna: Cotton fabric with printed paisley patterns. The bandanna can be used as a handkerchief but is most commonly worn around the neck or head.
Scarf: A quadrilateral or triangular piece of fabric worn around the neck or head. Thin fabric, such as silk, is used most often.
Shawl: Quadrilateral or triangular wool fabric worn around the neck or head for warmth. A shawl is larger than a scarf but smaller than a stole.
Stole: large shawl
Scarf: Rectangular piece of fabric used to keep warm. Wool, cashmere, and silk are the most common materials used.

18 Belts
An ornament worn around the waist to secure bottoms. Most belts are band shaped with a buckle. However, chains, beads, and strings are among the many variations available.

19 Hosiery
General term for socks and stockings. Looking at them from shortest to longest, we have socklets (ankle length), socks (above the ankle), crew socks (thigh length), high socks (just below the knee), knee-high socks (just above the knee), and panty stockings (waist height; thick panty stockings are called tights).

20 Leg Warmers
A type of hosiery. A knitted fabric that covers everything from the ankle to the knee.

21 Pocketchief
An ornamental handkerchief stored in the pocket. There are various ways of folding a pocketchief. The illustration here is an example of the crushed style of folding.

Chapter2
Design Ideas

The Three Pillars of Design

If you design clothes in an ambiguous manner, then you can think only within your own conventions and you end up producing the same forms over and over again. Always the same dress, always the same silhouette. . . . How does one break this habit and create a variety of high-quality design variations? Just remember: from large items to small items. That is to say, you should always consider working in the following the order: silhouette, parts, details. These are the three pillars of design. When you add different materials, patterns, and colors to the three pillars, there is no limit to what you can create.

Section 1 — The Process of Designing "Real Clothes"

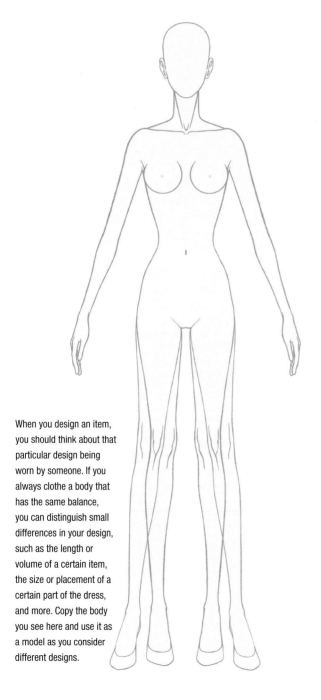

When you design an item, you should think about that particular design being worn by someone. If you always clothe a body that has the same balance, you can distinguish small differences in your design, such as the length or volume of a certain item, the size or placement of a certain part of the dress, and more. Copy the body you see here and use it as a model as you consider different designs.

Design Process for a Top

We will design a "regular shirt." Materials will consist of the standard broadcloth (p. 109) used for shirts. The design is very basic, but we will go over each step one at a time.

Decide on a Silhouette

This will determine the overall shape of the clothing. It will also determine the overall image, so it is very important.

(Length)

First is the balance of the top and the bottom, which is to say you need to determine the overall shirt length. (See "Length Variations: Tops," p. 34.)

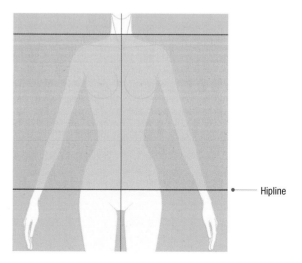

Hipline

1 Since this is a standard shirt, you will measure things to the hipline. (See "Length Variations: Tops," p. 34.)

The tip of the shoulder ⟶ ⟵ The point of the shoulder

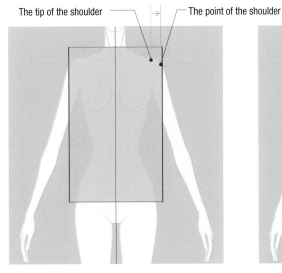
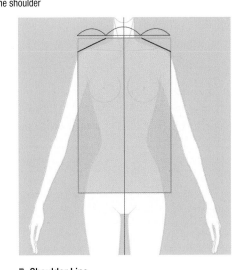

Outline

Next you decide on the width. Setting the width is the same as setting the size of the garment.

2 Dresses and shirts with sleeves will not have any freedom of movement if there is not enough width to them, so you should measure sleeves from the tip of the shoulder, not from the point of the shoulder.

3 Shoulder Line
Here is a simple shoulder line for a shirt without shoulder pads. Break the width into three parts and draw in the shoulder line. The shoulder line should have room. (See "Shoulder Line," p. 56.)

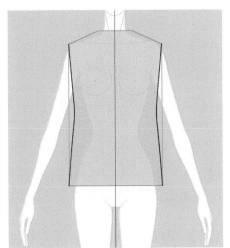

4 Outline
Here we have given the design a little more shape. The trick to enhancing the length of the leg is to put the waistline of the top a little higher than the actual waistline. (See "Outline Variations," pp. 34–35.)

Structural Lines

For people to wear clothes in a nonlinear manner, you need to sew the cloth three-dimensionally; thus, structural lines are unavoidable. For women, the bust will bulge somewhat and the waist will be constricted. Think of these two points when putting in the darts and panel lines.

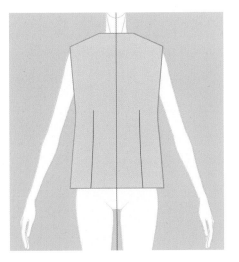
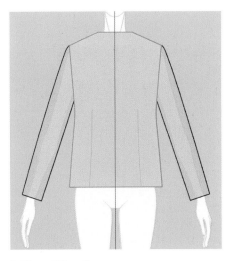

5 Since we took in the waist, we will also put in front darts. (See "Structural Line: Tops," p. 38.)

6 Sleeve Silhouette
We made them tight.

Decide on Parts

Begin designing each of the parts that will make up each item. The eye-catching neck area is the best place to begin.

Design of the Collar

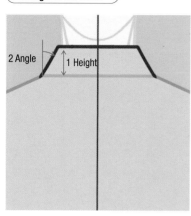

2 Angle 1 Height

7 First of all, decide on the back collar height.

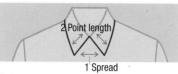

1 Top

8 Neckline
Since this is a shirt, you should first decide upon the cut of the V-zone.
Draw a V shape from the top of the back collar.
(See p. 42 for variations in neckline design.)

2 Point length

1 Spread

9 Draw the spread of the collar points and the distance from the collar band to the collar point.

10 Since this is a fairly high collar, we decided to attach a collar base.
Now the design of the collar is complete.
(See p. 46 for variations in collar design.)

Hemline Design

11 We elected to use a tailed bottom for the hemline on this one.
The back of the bodice is longer.
Here, we assumed that the shirt would be worn while occasionally bending over.
(See p. 65 for "Variations on Tops: Hemline.")

Front Design

12 Placket Front
We made it a French front.
(See p. 52 for variations in placket front design.)

13 Buttons
The key points for buttons are their size and number. First, decide on the position of the top and bottom button. Be sure to draw the buttonholes as well. Draw vertical buttonholes for an innerwear (shirts, blouses, etc.) and horizontal buttonholes for outerwear (jackets, coats, etc.). Since the grain line of the collar base is horizontal, the buttonhole on the collar base is going to be horizontal as well.

14 Last, evenly allocate the rest of the buttons.
(See p. 52 for variations in body front design.)

Sleeve Design

15 First, erase the sideline. The erased area will become the armhole.

16 Choose a shirt sleeve for the armhole.
(See p. 57 for variations in armhole design.)

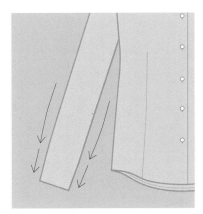

17 Design the Sleeve
Choose a long sleeve that narrows at the cuff.
(See p. 58 for variations in sleeve design.)

18 Design the cuff(s).
Decide on the height of the cuff.

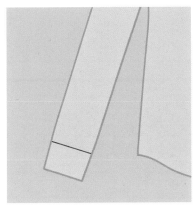

19 In order to add details on the cuff, be sure to draw the backside of the cuff. Copy the front to make the height of the backside the same as the front.

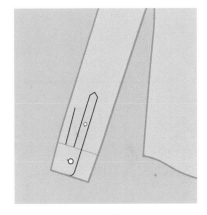

20 Sleeve Placket and Buttons
Add a sleeve placket and make the buttons one size smaller than those on the front.
(See p. 61 for variations in cuff design.)

Back Design

21 Draw the collar and yoke.

22 Add a center box pleat.

Decide on Details

"Detail" is the general term for the fine elements on a garment.

23 Add a yoke on the shoulders for reinforcement. The grain line of the yoke should be horizontal.
(See p. 67 for variations in yoke design.)

24 Pocket

First, map out a quadrilateral shape to check balance. Then add detail.
(See p. 73 for design variations for pockets on tops.)

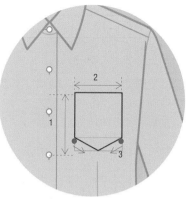

1 Use the position of the button as a gauge.
2 This particular pocket uses the space from the second to the fourth buttons.
3 Make the pocket relatively wide.

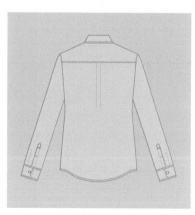

25 Last, add stitches to tighten up the design. (See p. 75 for variations in stitch design.)

26 Complete

Design Process for a Skirt

Designing a "gored skirt." Here, we chose chiffon (see p. 111), which is commonly used for skirts.

Decide on a Silhouette

Decide the overall form of the garment. The silhouette is crucial because it influences the overall image of the garment.

Length

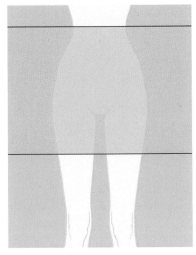

Outline

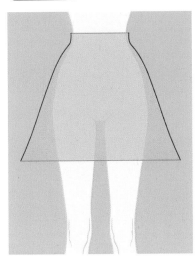

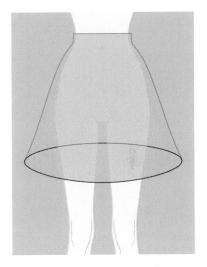

1 First, determine the vertical balance. This particular design has a natural waistline and miniskirt length for the hemline.
(See p. 36 for "Length Variations: Skirts.")

2 Next, design the outline of the skirt while remaining cognizant of the flare in the skirt. We chose a loose flare here.
(See p. 36 for the outline variations.)

3 Since the skirt is supposed to be puffy, we made the hemline oval in order to bring out a three-dimensional feel.

Structural Lines

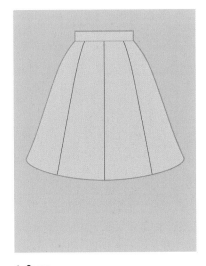

4 Waistline
The waistband is called a "separate waistband."

5 Opening
We placed the opening at the back.

6 Gores
The skirt is puffy, so we made it an eight-gored skirt.
(See p. 41 for variations in structural line.)

Decide on Your Parts

Design each part that makes up the item.

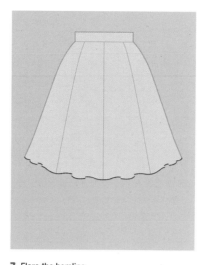

7 Flare the hemline.
(See p. 66 for "Variations on Bottoms: Hemline.")

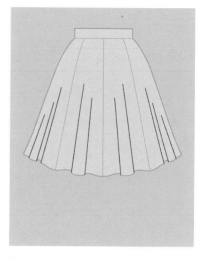

8 Add creases to the flared portions.

Decide on the Details

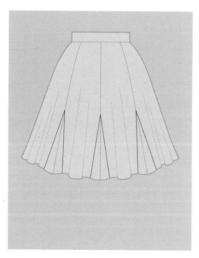

9 Add gores to accentuate the puffiness of the skirt (p. 72).
(See pp. 71 and 72 for variations in detail design.)

10 Complete

Design Process for Pants

We will be designing jeans. Of course, the fabric is denim (p. 109).

Decide on a Silhouette

Determine the overall shape of the garment. This process is crucial because it will influence the overall image of the garment.

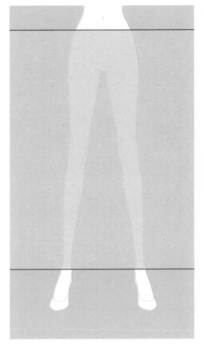

Length

1 First, determine the vertical balance.
We elected to have a low-rise waist and long length.
(See p. 37 for "Length Variations: Pants.")

Outline

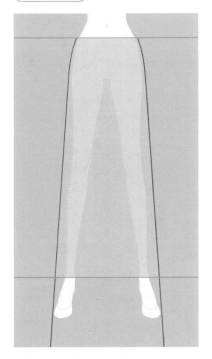

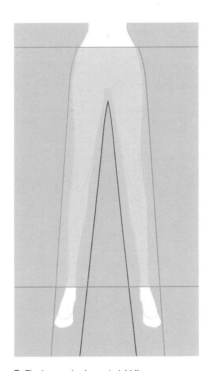

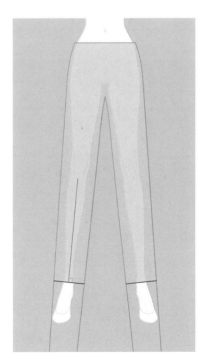

2 Next, design the outline while considering the width of the pants. This particular design uses a straight line.

3 The inseam is also a straight line. (See p. 37 for outline variations.)

4 Adjust the hemline according to the silhouette. Make it perpendicular to the grain line of the pants.

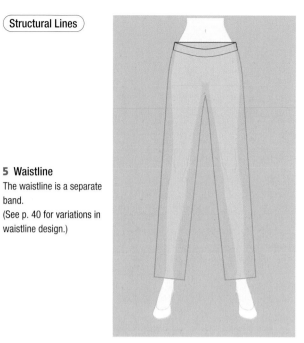

5 Waistline
The waistline is a separate band.
(See p. 40 for variations in waistline design.)

6 Opening
The opening is a fly front.

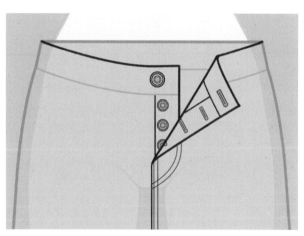

7 We made it a button fly.
(See p. 40 for variations in fly front design.)

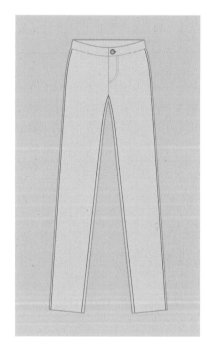

8 The front has no pleat. Since we made the front shallow, for ease of movement, we need to add lines for the side seam and the inseam.
(See p. 41 for variations in pleats.)

Decide on Parts

Design each part that makes up the item one by one.

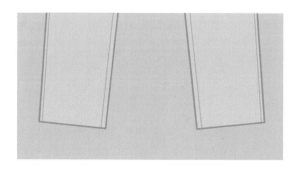

9 The hem is single cuffed.
(See p. 66 for "Variations on Bottoms: Hemline.")

Decide on the Details

10 Add belt loops.

11 Add pockets. This particular design is an L-pocket. (See p. 74 for "Design Variation of Pockets Found on Pants.")

12 We attached a coin pocket on the right.

13 Reinforce the mouth of the pocket with rivets.

14 Attach a yoke.

15 The back style looks like this. Seen from the back, the yoke looks like this.

16 Add belt loops to the back.

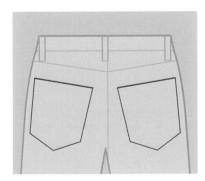

17 Add the hip pockets.

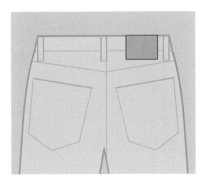

18 Attach a leather patch.

19 Reinforce the ends of the stitching with bar tacks (see p. 72).

20 Add bar tacks where material can easily fray, such as the pocket.

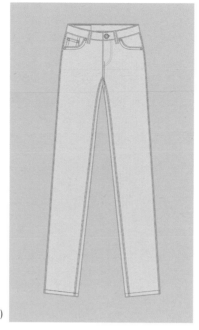

21 Add stitches.
(See pp. 67 to 72 for variations in details design.)

22 Stitches on the hip pockets are key points for showing originality.

23 Complete

Front style

Back style

Design Process for Headwear

Hat

1 If your imagination isn't in overdrive, try drawing your design on an illustration of a face instead of just drawing your hat design.

2 Make the shoulder (p. 79) of the hat oval shaped. Draw the shoulder while considering the angle at which the hat should be worn.

3 Draw a guideline for creating the side crown (p. 79) of the hat. Drop a perpendicular line from the center of the oval to help with your drawing.

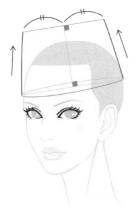

4 Determine how the crown of the hat will fit the head.
Decide on a design where the crown of the hat becomes narrow toward the top.

5 Draw the tip (p. 79) of the hat in an oval shape.
This will help determine the height of the crown.

6 Draw the edge of the brim (p. 79).

7 Draw the angle of the brim (p. 79). Any hat with a downward-sloping brim is called a "cloche."

8 Like a pork pie hat, if the brim curves up, the edge of the brim goes above the shoulder of the hat.

9 Draw the curve of the brim.

10 Make the edge of the brim parallel to the shoulder.

11 Like with a soft hat, if the front of the brim faces downward and the back of the brim curves upward, it is better to draw the edge of the hat at an angle.

12 The angle of the brim goes downward from the shoulder of the hat and then curves upward at the back.

13 Make the edge of the brim parallel to the shoulder of the hat.

14 Draw the hatband.
1 Decide on a width.
2 Make it parallel to the shoulder of the hat.

15 Draw the center crease.

16 Draw the center dent.

17 Decide on a color and then complete. For this particular design, we chose a chic black.

Cap

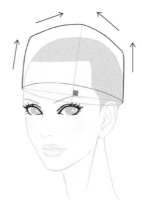

1 Make the shoulder of the cap an oval shape. Draw while considering the angle at which the hat should be worn.

2 Draw a guideline in order to draw the side crown of the cap. Drop a perpendicular line down from the center of the oval to help with drawing.

3 Determine how the crown of the hat will fit the head. We decided on a design where the crown of the hat becomes narrow toward the top. We also made the top crown a chevron shape.

4 Determine the length of the peak.

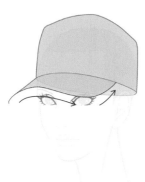

5 Draw the contours of the peak. There are two types of peak: squared and rounded. This particular style has a squared peak.

6 Draw the sandwich of the cap and the top button.

7 There are two types of crown: six gored and eight gored. This particular design is six gored.

8 An eyelet is attached to each gore. Then, add stitches. The stitch on the peak has the purpose of maintaining the shape of the peak.

9 Since the intention here was to make a "back mesh" cap, we drew a sweatband that you can see through. The sweatband is partially attached to the inside of the cap.

10 Draw mesh.

11 Set the color scheme. We selected white and pink.

12 Add a logo to complete.

Bibliography:
Fashion Dictionary (Bunka Publishing Bureau),
Japanese English Fashion Term Dictionary (Senken Shimbun-sha),
New Fashion Business Fundamental Term Encyclopedia (Chanera),
Styling Book (Graphic-sha)

The examples introduced here were just a group of simple items. Still, they took form by examining each item closely and designing them step by step. Let's start coming up with cool variations by combining various silhouettes, parts, and details.

Section 2 Deconstruction and Reconstruction of an Item

When I design an item, I begin taking it apart piece by piece. What kind of possibilities are out there to make an existing form even more beautiful? It is crucial to examine every single element that makes up a garment. In this section, let's conceive of a design using a trench coat.

Setting the Theme

Trench Coat Details

Epaulet

Storm patch

Double breasted

Flap pocket

Napoleonic collar

Belt

D ring

Cuff strap

First of all, let's start with the origin of the trench coat. It was used by the British army in World War I because it was a durable coat that could tolerate battles in the "trench." The British companies Burberry and Aquascutum are said to be the original creators of the trench coat. Since the design is filled with functional beauty and is also highly practical, the trench coat became a very popular fashion item among hard-boiled fiction enthusiasts. In recent years, there is a trend toward creating ladies' fashions on the basis of reinventing men's fashion items. So, in this section, let's give it a try by turning a trench coat into a ladies' one-piece dress.

As far as the details are concerned, we must remember that certain things, in particular the Napoleonic collar and the double breast, cannot be modified or we will no longer have a trench coat. So, let's proceed with the deconstruction and reconstruction while remaining cognizant of those two details.

Method of Design

Silhouette

When your design stands by itself as an item, you must reconsider its silhouette (both length and width) even if changes have already been made to that silhouette.

Details

Beyond simply protecting the body, fashion in the modern era seeks to create beauty within a garment.

Thus, we can choose to ignore some of the functional and practical details found in the original garment, and then we can reexamine the design and make it our own. There are three ways to do this:

Rearrange

Resize

Overdecorate

Design Sketch

First, make a copy of the original item you wish to redesign. Develop your design as you trace the copy over.

On a large piece of paper, try to freely develop your design.

The Silhouette

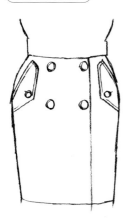

Chosen design

Since I saw a number of possibilities for developing designs on the bottom part of the coat, I began there. The first idea I had was for a cocoon line. It has a mature look.

Next, I moved on to the flare line. Since a girlish feel is naturally brought out in this skirt, I chose to use this design.

Napoleonic Collar

triple

We will use this.

Then, I looked at the details. The key point here is to begin designing with the collar. I attempted to make a three-layered lapel.

I also attempted to create a deep V-zone cut on the petal collar. We will use this design.

Front

belt →

Use the epaulet as a belt loop.

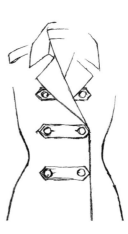

"Resize" and "rearrange" the details and then attach the cuff straps to the front.

I brought the back belts to the front.

A D ring is a clip for attaching a hand grenade. In recent years the D ring has been omitted, so I decided to bring it back.

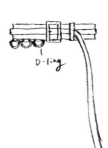

D-ling

I chose this design.

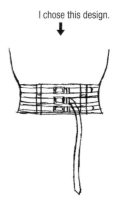

"Overdecorate": attach layers to the pockets.

Also, "overdecorate" a belt.

I attached triple-stranded thin belts over a thick belt. We will use this design.

fur

leather

I selected silk for our material. I was considering the sparing use of laces, but I eventually chose to design using leather and fur instead.
After all, leather and fur will bring about a certain "thickness" in the design.

(Sleeves)

Since sleeves influence the silhouette of the garment, I always design them carefully. I elected the leg-of-mutton sleeve with "overdecorated" cuff straps and then added drapes. It looks a little gaudy.

Wrap the cuff straps around the three-quarter sleeve.

It could be sleeveless.

↑
Use this.

The American sleeve and the epaulet are reversed. I made a glove with a cuff strap.

Puff sleeve. Simple yet cute. I chose this design.

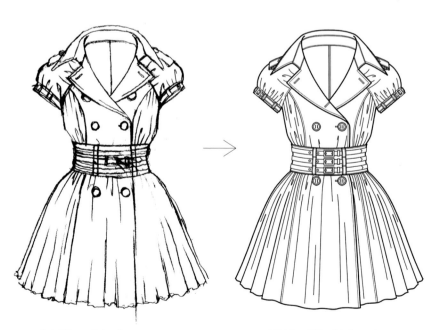

Put all the parts together.
Our rough sketch is complete.

Add ink: add fine details, such as stiches, with a pen.

Design Sketch

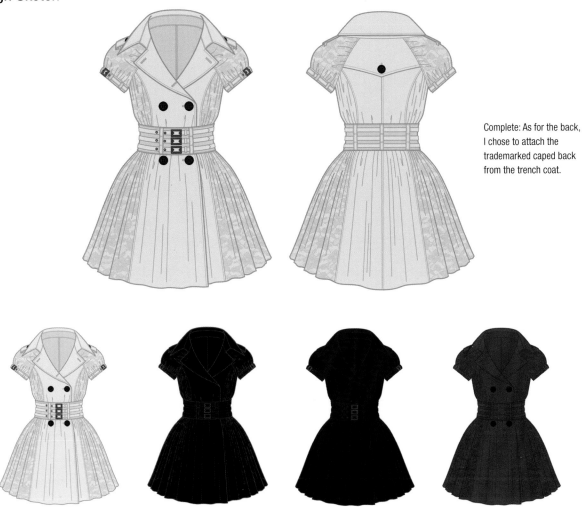

Complete: As for the back, I chose to attach the trademarked caped back from the trench coat.

Color variations: First, let's fill with basic colors used in clothing. Basic clothing colors consist of beige, because it matches some skin colors fairly well; brown and navy, because they emphasize the transparency and luminosity of skin; and an achromatic color (white, black, or gray). These colors look good on anyone, regardless of age or sex.

You must also consider the color scheme specific to this item. Since this garment is for spring and summer, I decided to use pale colors. The sheer look of the garment suits this choice.

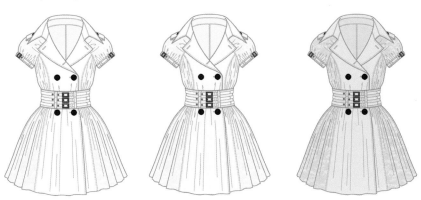

I hope we accurately demonstrated how important it is to reexamine each individual part to understand all of the characteristics of the silhouette. Let's try to deconstruct and reconstruct other items.

Section **3** Creative Designs

When you design a garment to conform to a single theme, the overall image of the garment becomes very important. Therefore, when using a single theme you should begin by looking at the overall design, rather taking the item apart piece by piece.

Basing Ideas off the Silhouette

Design a Silhouette

This time the theme is a "water drop." Be sure to envision the silhouette as you consider new ideas.

1

Silhouette 1:
A simple oval

Silhouette 2:
A hanging water drop

Silhouette 3:
A water drop deformed by the wind

Silhouette 4:
A hanging water drop being blown by the wind as it elongates

We will go with this one.

Determine the Size and Volume

Determine how the silhouette is worn on the body. The image will change depending on the size and proportion of the silhouette that covers the mannequin.

2 A mannequin:
Since the silhouettes have "movement" on both sides, we tried putting them over a mannequin that is standing at an angle.

3

← We will go with this one.

Style 1
Covers the neck to the thigh. This is the most standard style.

Style 2
Here we attempted to cover the entire body. This is the most adverse style.

Style 3
We attempted to cover the body like a long dress. It is difficult to bring out the rhythmic flow within.

Style 4
Entirely covers the upper body. Since the design around the face seems as though it could turn into something interesting, I chose this one.

Let's Develop a New Item   Develop a design while making use of the silhouette.

Design Sketch

4 At first, draw a silhouette and then divide the item into individual parts after adjusting the overall balance.

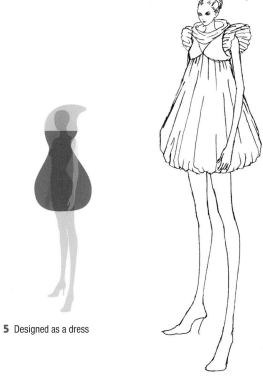

5 Designed as a dress

I tried turning the silhouette into a hairstyle around the face. It's cute but not that interesting.

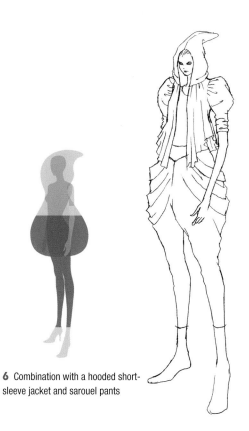

6 Combination with a hooded short-sleeve jacket and sarouel pants

We brought out more volume by attaching straps to the pants.

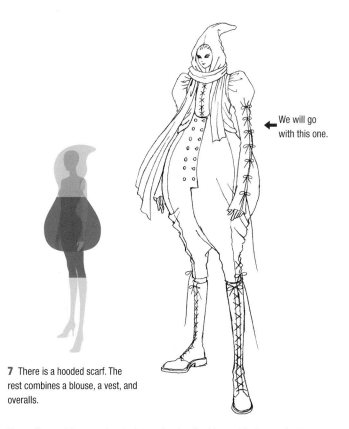

← We will go with this one.

7 There is a hooded scarf. The rest combines a blouse, a vest, and overalls.

The puffiness of the pants is quite interesting. I prefer this one. The lace-up boots are also a key point.

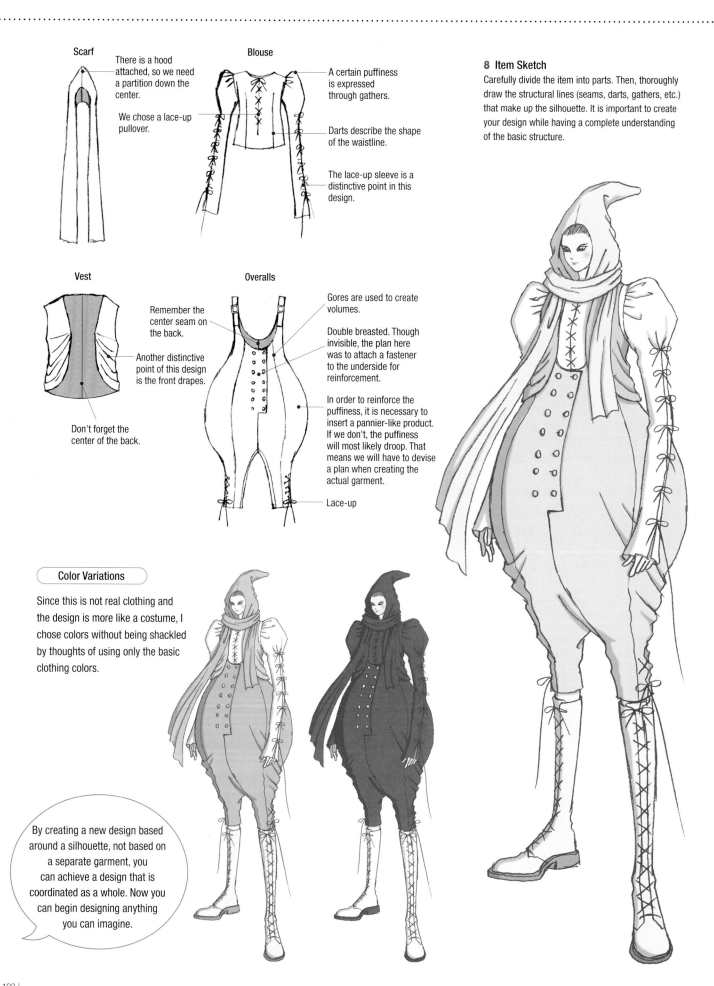

Scarf

There is a hood attached, so we need a partition down the center.

We chose a lace-up pullover.

Blouse

A certain puffiness is expressed through gathers.

Darts describe the shape of the waistline.

The lace-up sleeve is a distinctive point in this design.

Vest

Remember the center seam on the back.

Another distinctive point of this design is the front drapes.

Don't forget the center of the back.

Overalls

Gores are used to create volumes.

Double breasted. Though invisible, the plan here was to attach a fastener to the underside for reinforcement.

In order to reinforce the puffiness, it is necessary to insert a pannier-like product. If we don't, the puffiness will most likely droop. That means we will have to devise a plan when creating the actual garment.

Lace-up

8 Item Sketch

Carefully divide the item into parts. Then, thoroughly draw the structural lines (seams, darts, gathers, etc.) that make up the silhouette. It is important to create your design while having a complete understanding of the basic structure.

(Color Variations)

Since this is not real clothing and the design is more like a costume, I chose colors without being shackled by thoughts of using only the basic clothing colors.

By creating a new design based around a silhouette, not based on a separate garment, you can achieve a design that is coordinated as a whole. Now you can begin designing anything you can imagine.

Conceiving an Idea Based on a Motif

Let's Find a Motif

The world around us is filled with different shapes. Inspiration can be found in creations of nature—animals, plants, and scenery—and man-made objects, including architecture, computers, cell phones, cars, books, audio and visual equipment, and more.

By observing objects that are seemingly totally unrelated to clothes at first glance, you can deepen your appreciation for "forms."

1 I picked a bottle that I found in my house as a motif. I wanted to successfully re-create the rhythmic flow created by its straight and curved lines.

Design Sketch

A key point here is to decide which part of your item will employ the motif. We will attempt to look at the motif from various angles and use it to create silhouettes of entire garments or just details.

*The pink portion of the motif (in the photo box) is used for designing.

Item

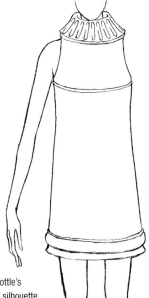

2 Dress
The flared-out portion of the bottle turned into accordion pleats here.

3 Dress
Here we used the shape of the bottle's body as is. The sheath line is the silhouette. One distinctive element here is the collar. It comes from the beginning of the bottle's neck.

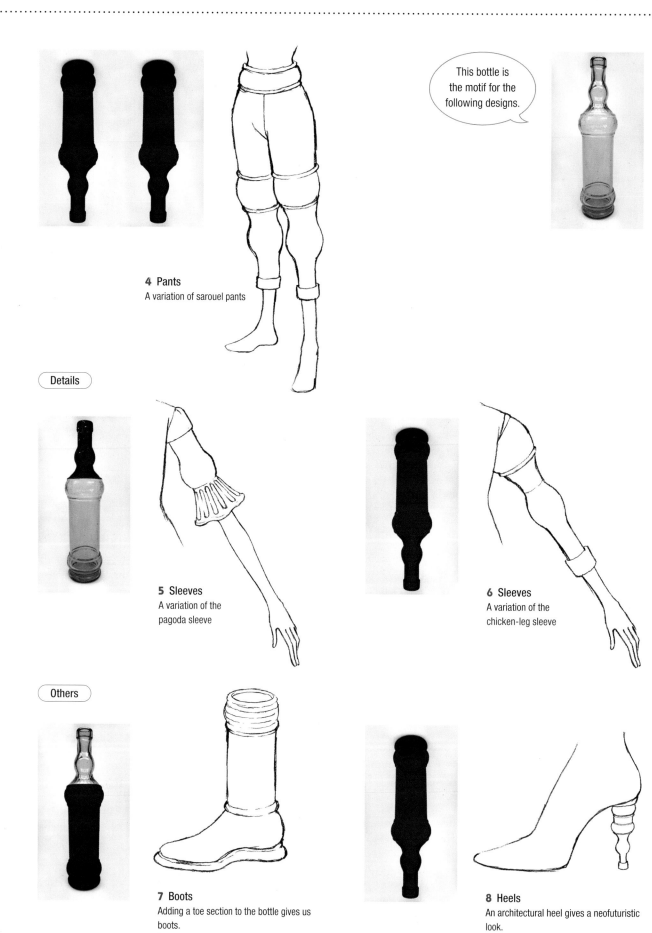

This bottle is the motif for the following designs.

4 Pants
A variation of sarouel pants

Details

5 Sleeves
A variation of the pagoda sleeve

6 Sleeves
A variation of the chicken-leg sleeve

Others

7 Boots
Adding a toe section to the bottle gives us boots.
The distinctive features of the boots are the roundness of the mouth and the sole.

8 Heels
An architectural heel gives a neofuturistic look.

Drawing Inspiration from Paintings

In 1965, Yves Saint Laurent introduced "the Mondrian Collection." It has been said that the painting collection of Piet Mondrian, a Dutch painter, was the source of inspiration for this collection.

> If you are lacking a source of inspiration, it might be a good idea to paint one for yourself.

Painting

1 Even though I used opaque watercolors (I used Nicker Designer Colours), there are really no specific materials or colors that must be used. I do recommend that you prepare separate brushes for each color.

2 Without really thinking dircctly about clothing, you should just move your brush around however you like.

3 In order to paint even more instinctively, I attempted to paint holding three brushes— for red, blue, and yellow—at once. It could be interesting to even try finger painting.

4 Complete

Planning

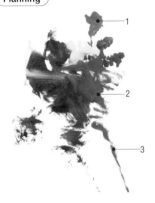 

5 Look at your finished painting from different angles. By slightly tilting to the left, I started to see 1 as a face, 2 as clothes, and 3 as legs. I could see an image where a person is leaping toward the right.

6 By tilting the image further, it started to look like a flared dress. I decided to omit the portion marked with an X. I have an image in my head of 1 being ribbons that wrap around an arm.

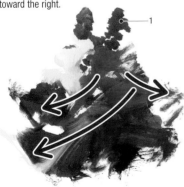  

7 The image above is after the unnecessary parts have been removed. 1 can be turned into a collar. The arrows show the flow within a garment as a whole. I intended to express that flow by using details.

8 Once your image is solidified, cut the painting out and paste it onto a croquis.

9 Prepare a croquis. I decided to use the walking croquis from p. 126. Make enlargements or scaled-down copies of your painting in order to match them with your croquis.

10 If you have a computer, you can scan your painting and process it using Photoshop (use a resolution over 200). First, copy your painting over an image of the croquis. The painting layer is shown in blue. That layer is hiding the lower portion of the croquis.

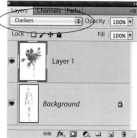

11 In the menu bar, select "Window" and then click "Layer" to open the Layer Palette. Then, change the mode from "Normal" to "Darken" in order to make the body of the croquis visible.

12 The croquis is now visible.

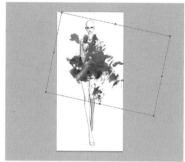
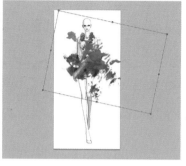

13 Select "Edit" in the menu bar and then select "Transform" (command + T). While the handle is a double-headed arrow, rotate the layer by dragging to change the angle. Also, drag the handle while holding down the shift key to enable scaling and to distort the layer while keeping the aspect ratio.

14 Complete: now we have the same result as the cut-and-paste version.

Design

15 Draw a rough sketch of the item. Begin with a silhouette. Carefully observe the painting to grasp its distinctive features. The intention here was to re-create a silhouette with a fitted bodice that flares out at the hem.

16 Think about the details. The large and small belts on the sides of the dress droop and bring out a heaviness in the garment, so I chose to use lots of chiffon frills to offset that effect.

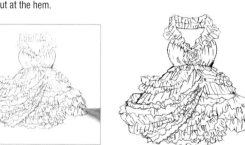

17 Add other details. Proceed to create the garment while thinking about the colors you will use and the brushstrokes. Widening of the skirt is expressed through overlapping tiers.

18 Complete

Now you see that anything and everything around you can be used for fashion inspiration. And now you can expand your design abilities by using themes from a huge variety of motifs.

Chapter 3
Textiles

What Are Textiles...?

Materials and patterns

Excluding a small number of photos, those listed in this chapter are scaled down to 40 percent. When drawing a B4-size design sketch (257 x 364 mm / 10⅛″ x 14¼″), we recommended using a photo that is further reduced by half. The photos that are labeled with "(20 percent)" are reduced only 20 percent in order to show patterns more clearly. These photos are sized to correspond to B4-size design sketches (257 x 364 mm / 10⅛″ x 14¼″).

Cloth

Woven fabric. This fabric in general is made by interchangeably weaving the warp yarn and the weft yarn. Generally, cloth doesn't stretch out when pulled, as opposed to knitted fabrics.

Yarn size

The size of the yarn actually tends to determine the overall shape of a garment. It is very important because it influences the overall image greatly.

Cotton count
A unit that indicates the size of yarn

A skein material weight of 1 pound (approximately 454 g) for 840 yards of yarn (approximately 768 m) is equal to 1 cotton count. At the same weight, if the length of the yarn is twice the 840 yards, the cotton count will be 2. If the length is triple the 840 yards, the cotton count is 3, and so on and so forth. Popular counts for yarns are 48 count (weight 1 kg and 48 km long) for worsted yarn, and 14 count for a single yarn that makes 60 count two-ply woolen yarn. For cotton, single yarn of 20 or 40 count is the most common. Denims range between 10 and 14 count. Poplins are 30 to 50 count. Broadcloth uses thin yarn that is 60 count or more. The higher the count gets, the thinner and smoother the woven fabric gets. This results in a high-quality textile.

Denier
A unit that measures the mass of fibers or filaments

A 9,000-meter strand of filament that weighs about 1 gram is 1 denier. So, this is in opposition to the cotton count system, since the number of the denier gets larger as the yarn becomes thicker. Denoted with an S, the denier count is indicated as 60s (20-count single yarn) or 60 s/2 (60-count two-ply yarn). Two-ply yarn is a yarn made by twisting two separate strands of yarn together.

Cloth (woven fabric): three foundation weaves

Methods of weaving are largely categorized into three different methods.

Plain weave
The most simple weaving. The warp and weft are aligned interchangeably. It has crisp texture. Examples are broadcloth, lawn, oxford, taffeta, georgette, etc.

Twill
A fabric where either the warp or the weft is ribbed, and the weave runs diagonally (in this direction /). Compared to a plain weave, twill has a supple texture and a few of other merits, including that it is not easily wrinkled and that it has excellent elasticity. Examples are denim, dungaree, flannel (cotton flannel), drill, gabardine, serge, etc.

Satin weave
This textile minimizes the intersection of the warp and the weft as much as possible, and where intersections do occur, they are random. Thus, there is warp-faced satin, where the warp yarn is ribbed, and weft-faced satins, where the weft yarn is ribbed. Satin is lustrous, flexible, and soft to the touch. Satin is, of course, the most well-known example of this type of weave.

1. Natural Fiber
A general term for fibers made from plants, animals, minerals, etc.

Plant-based fiber
Any natural fiber created from plants

Seed Fiber

Fibers that are taken from the seeds of plants; for example, cotton

1 Broadcloth (Broad)
Lustrous plain-weave fabric that is typically found in dress shirts. The thinner the yarn, the greater the quality of the fabric. High-quality broadcloth has a silklike texture. Other term: poplin.

2 Oxford
A somewhat coarse, plain-weaved fabric. A relatively thick cotton fabric that breathes well, this is the fabric of choice for classic button-down shirts, the majority of which are pale in color (e.g., white or blue).

3 Denim
The opposite of dungaree, this is a twill fabric that uses indigo yarn for the warp and either plain white or unbleached yarn for the weft. In recent years, however, denim has not been strictly distinguished from dungarees. Instead, dungaree tends to use thin fabric, while denim uses thick fabric. This method of distinguishing dungaree and denim has become the standard. Also, yarns that are not dyed indigo blue can still be called denim. For example, there is white denim, black denim, etc.

4 Chambray
A plain-weave fabric that uses colored yarn (indigo) for the warp and either unbleached or plain white yarn for the weft. Chambray has a specific marbling pattern and tends to be a thin fabric.

5 Dungaree
A twill fabric that uses either unbleached or plain white yarn for the warp and indigo yarn for the weft. Thicker than chambray.

6 Chino Cloth
A plain-weave fabric that is thicker than broadcloth. Chino is the material in chino pants.

7 Katsuragi
A thick twill fabric that is often used for work clothes

8 Suede Cloth
A single-sided, brushed fabric that mimics suede

9 Burberry
A type of cotton gabardine and waterproof fabric developed by Burberry in London. Elaborate and lustrous, this is a high-quality fabric that has excellent texture.

10 Corduroy
A cotton material with vertical cords. Fabrics with narrow cords (fine corduroy) are good for shirts, while fabrics with thick cords (elephant corduroy) are used for pants and jackets.

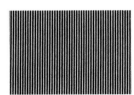

11 Cordlane
Fabric used for summer clothes. Its thin, vertical ridge-like stripes are distinctive.

12 Piqué
The wale (vertical column of stitches) is wide. Besides cotton, piqué in silk and rayon is also available.

13 Dobby Cloth (Dobby Stripe)
A fabric that has fine and consecutive weave patterns

14 Voile
A thin, sheer fabric

15 Velvet

The warp makes a pile. This is a vertical-pile, plush fabric. Filament yarn* materials, such as silk and rayon, are used. *Filament yarn has long, continuous fibers. For instance, silk has a single fiber that is very long and continuous. The opposite is spun yarn (short fiber).

16 Velveteen

This time the weft yarn makes the pile. Velveteen is a horizontal-pile fabric using short yarn. Cotton velveteen and corduroy have a similar structure.

17 Velour

Originally a Latin word meaning hairy. This fabric is categorized into three types, as described below.
① Knitted velour: a nap-like short velveteen is created by shearing plush pile.
② As a synonym for plush: This is a fabric that exposes a long nap by shearing the pile. Velour has a long and thick nap compared to velvet.
③ A woolen fabric with a velour finish: this is used for making dresses and coats.

18 Poplin

A plain-weave fabric that has fine horizontal wales, where the wales are wider than broadcloth

19 Ripple

A fabric with puckered ripples. Ripple has various puckered shapes. By contrast, seersucker has only stripes.

20 Lawn

A thin and fine fabric that uses 60-to-80-cotton-count yarn for the warp and 80-to-100-cotton-count yarn for the weft. Originally made from linen, now lawn is mainly cotton.

21 Gauze

A coarse, plain-weave fabric. Light and soft. Also, it absorbs moisture well.

22 Crêpe

A fabric that has a crimped surface. The fine, uneven surface of the fabric makes up the crimped appearance.

23 *Yoryu*-crêpe

The crimp runs vertically, like stripes.

24 Crinkle Process

A fabric that is processed to mimic crêpe by washing until the fabric becomes wrinkled

25 Quilted

A sewn material that is designed to secure batting (feathers, cotton, etc.) laid down between two pieces of fabric

Bast Fiber

A fiber collected from the stems of plants

26 Linen (Flax)
Highly durable and absorbs moisture well, but it also wrinkles easily. Commonly, "linen" means flax fiber. Produced in both Belgium and the Netherlands (Courtrai linen). Both are known as high-quality linen. Other fibers, such as jute, hemp, ramie, etc., are also used.

Vein Fiber

Fibers collected from plant leaves. Not suited for clothing. Examples include Manila hemp, burlap, etc.

Animal fibers   Fibers collected from animals

Silk

A fabric made from the cocoons of silkworms. This fabric has the most elegant luster.

1 Chiffon
Made from single yarns of raw silk that are coarsely plain-weaved. It is a thin and soft silk fabric.

2 Organdy
A thin, lightweight, sheer plain-weave fabric. It has a distinctive stiff texture and luster.

3 Satin
A satin weave fabric that is smooth and glossy

4 Taffeta
A plain-weave fabric with very fine horizontal wales. The warp is very tight, while the weft uses a slightly thick yarn.

5 *Fuji* Silk
Originally, this is a trademarked name of Fuji Spinning. When compared to Habutae (see right), Fuji silk has a subtle luster.

6 *Habutae*
A lustrous, smooth-textured, plain-woven fabric. Variations include twill and satin.

7 *Crêpe de chine*
Means "crêpe from China" in French. Its distinctive features include a supple, fine crinkle.

8 Georgette (Georgette Crêpe)
A crinkled fabric that has a sheer, crisp texture. The texture is actually slightly stiff. Aside from plain weave, there is also satin georgette and crêpe (similar to the peel of a pear, it is a weave that has a fine, uneven surface).

9 Moire
A fabric with a wavy appearance

10 Shantung
The name originates from Shandong Province in China, where silk is spun from Chinese oak-feeding silkworm cocoons. Slabs seen on a surface are its distinctive feature.

Wool

Fabric collected from the coats of sheep. Worsted woolens are thin, long, and smooth, while tweed is thick, short, and coarse. In the broad sense, fabrics collected from goats, camels, and rabbits are also considered wool.
Other term: lana.

Worsted

1 Gabardine
A fine and durable twill. The angle of the twill weave is 60 degrees. It has superior durability and heat retention. Besides wool, we also find gabardine in cotton, linen, polyester, etc.

2 Serge
Serge is the most practical woolen twill. The angle of the twill weave is 45 degrees.

3 Kersey
A very durable thick twill. Characteristics include visible wales. Used for army uniforms and items that require durability.

4 Doeskin
The surface mimics doeskin and is a worsted five-harness satin. Slightly thick and glossy, doeskin is the highest-quality wool, and it is used for formal wear.

5 Tropical
Uses high-cotton-count yarn to make a coarse, plain-weave fabric. Representative of summer wool and characterized by a lightweight, crisp texture.

6 Sharkskin
Twilled fabric that alternately uses plain-white yarn and colored yarn for the warp and weft. The nap on the surface is removed to a clear-cut finish. The name comes from the fact that the texture is similar to the skin of a shark.

7 French Twill
A thick twilled fabric made from worsted yarn that has subtle gloss. Its distinctive feature is its wide and slightly bulged acute-angle wales.

8 Venetian
A satin weave with worsted yarn. A smooth, glossy, thick fabric used for formal wear.

9 Poral
Summer wool with a crisp texture that breathes well. Plain-weave, worsted yarn.

Woolen (Tweed)

10 Flannel

A lightweight and soft woolen fabric. Flannel is a warm fabric because the surface is napped. When flannel is woven using cotton, it is called "cotton flannel," and it is used for plaid-patterned work shirts, for example.

11 Nep Tweed

Handwoven tweed, manufactured in County Donegal, Ireland. It uses a woolen single yarn with a cotton count between 3 and 5. It is a plain-weave fabric woven with a plain-white warp and colored nap weft.
Other term: Donegal tweed.

12 Shetland Tweed

A tweed fabric woven with worsted yarn that was collected from sheep from Scotland's Shetland Islands. It has a soft and full texture.

13 Harris Tweed

Wool tweed made in the Outer Hebrides in northwestern Scotland. It has a rough and thick texture.

14 Loop Tweed

A type of Harris tweed spun on Lewis Island in northwestern Scotland

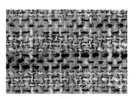

15 Fancy Tweed

Tweed that has different patterns and structures

16 Melton

Thick, soft woolen yarn is used for both the warp and weft. Wool fabric that has a sheared nap on the surface, this fabric is soft to the touch and very thick; thus, it is well suited to heavy winter clothing.

17 Birdseye

Small, round, white spots (like a bird's eye) are arranged all in a row.

18 Mossa

Moss-finished fabric

(Animal Hair Fiber)

Any fiber, except wool and silk, taken from animals

19 Cashmere

Cashmere is a goat fiber that is thin and soft. It is a top-quality product.

20 Mohair

A smooth, beautiful, lustrous white fiber obtained from the Angora goat. It has very long fibers and is used to weave high-quality materials.

21 Angora

Commonly uses Angora rabbit coats mixed with goat hair. Lightweight and warm. The term can also simply refer to Angora goat hair.

2. Synthetic fiber   A fiber that is chemically processed

Organic fiber   Any fiber made from plants, animals, and petroleum, among other organic materials

Regenerated Fiber

This is a fiber that is reconstructed from cellulose that has been dissolved in chemicals

1 Rayon (Viscose Rayon)
The raw material for rayon is pulp. It has a silklike luster and is easy to dye. However, rayon wrinkles easily.

2 Cupra
The raw material for cupra is cotton linter. It is dissolved in a cuprammonium solution to process. It is woven with very fine yarn and has a lustrous appearance.

Semisynthetic Fiber

A synthetic fiber synthesized using natural fiber materials

3 Acetate (Diacetate)
Its raw material is either linter pulp or wood pulp. Acetate is made from acetic anhydride and cellulose acetate that has an acetylation degree over 45 percent. Acetate has a silklike shine and texture. However, it is not as strong as silk.

4 Triacetate
Acetylation is over 59.5 percent. Similar to acetate, triacetate has a silklike glow and texture. Triacetate is higher in quality. It has superior heat resistance, but it lacks moisture absorbency.

5 Promix
Made from acrylonitrile and milk. It has a silklike, beautiful luster and texture.

Synthetic Fiber

A synthetic fiber made from organic substances such as petroleum, coal, limestone, etc.

6 Acrylic
Similar to wool, light and soft

9 Polyvinyl Chloride
Raw materials include coal, petroleum, and natural gas. It is charged with negative static electricity.

7 Polyester
The raw materials are petroleum, natural gas, etc. Sturdy and not easily wrinkled. Fast to dry, it lacks absorbency. Polyester is created by making full use of advanced technologies. New synthetic polyester has a unique texture and a high-quality feel that is better than simple polyester.

8 Nylon
Durable, lightweight, and not easily wrinkled. Used for hosiery, for example. First produced in the 1930s, nylon is well known as the first synthetic fiber invented in the world.

Knit

A single strand of yarn makes loops and is knit together to create a fabric. Knits have high elasticity, so this type of fabric is easier to use to make clothes that fit anyone's body, without relying heavily on structural lines.

The loops of yarn are connected in parallel to create a weft knit. By contrast, vertical loops create a warp knit.

Other term: jersey

*Gauge: number of stitches per 1.5″ (3.8 cm)

1 Low Gauge
Small gauge, such as 3 to 5. With low-gauge knits, it is necessary to use thick yarn.

2 Middle Gauge
6 to 10 gauge

3 Fine Gauge
This is a knit that uses extremely high-count yarn to create densely knitted stitches, even more so than high gauge.

The Weft Knitting

4 Single Jersey
Most basic structure for weft knitting. Used for T-shirts, for example.
Other term: cotton sheeting.

5 Rib Stitch
We can see that the wales are vertical in direction. This stitch is used for the collars and cuffs on sweaters and jackets.
Other term: ribbing.

Wrap Knitting

8 Tricot Knits
The stitches are doubled.

6 Purl Stitch
The surface is similar to single jersey, even though the back is pile. It is a thick fabric that has excellent heat retention properties. Used to make sweaters and parkas.

7 Interlock Stitch
A variation of the single jersey. The stitch pattern is distinctive. Used to make polo shirts.

9 Raschel Knits
Mesh-like knitted fabric. Used for nets and tulles.

Stitch

General term for loops and knitting methods

Variations of Fancy Stitching

1 Cable Stitch
A cable-like patterned stitch that is often seen in Aran sweaters and Tilden sweaters.
Other term: chain stitch.

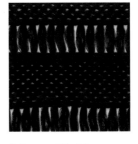

2 Lace and Eyelets
Like lace, a knitted fabric that has holes and is see-through

3 Jacquard Stitch
A knitted fabric that has obvious, raised patterns

Other Textiles

Lace   Has many gaps and patterned stitches

1 Tulle Lace
Tulle is a thin, netlike, hexagon-shaped stitch. Adding patterns creates tulle lace.

2 Chemical Lace
The patterns are made through chemical treatment.

Pattern Variations

Stripes   In the narrow sense, "stripes" refers to vertical stripes.

Material: Cotton

1 Pinstripe
The narrowest striping pattern available

2 Pencil Stripe
A pattern not unlike thin stripes that were drawn with a pencil. Narrower than a chalk stripe and wider than a pinstripe.

3 London Stripe
A striped pattern where the width of both the ground color and the stripes is the same. London stripes that are relatively wide are called block stripes.

Material: Wool

10 Herringbone
A striped pattern that mimics the shape of herring bones

4 Hairline Stripe
Narrow, vertical stripes that are arranged quite close together

5 Chalk Stripe
A narrow stripe that looks like it was drawn with chalk

6 Double Stripe
A paired-stripe pattern

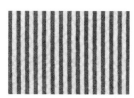

7 Seersucker (Sucker)
A cotton fabric that has wavelike puckers on the surface. Usually for sport shirts. Characterized by white and single-color stripes.

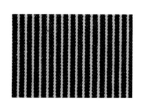

8 Hickory (Hickory Stripe)
A twill cotton fabric with a normal stripe pattern. Often used for making work shirts and overalls.

9 Border
A horizontal stripe pattern

Plaids (Tartan)

Material: Cotton

11 Gingham
A fine, plaid-patterned fabric with a plain-weave, high-count dyed yarn and bleached yarn

12 Madras Plaid (20 percent)
A striped pattern where the width of both the ground color and the stripes is the same

14 Tartan (20 percent)
Originally woven in Scotland, this is a plaid pattern associated with Scottish clans. It was used among prestigious families as a family crest and passed down for generations. Tartan patterns are fixed by each clan individually. It is estimated that there are over one hundred patterns. A thick material, such as cotton flannel, is most often used for tartan.

13 Block Plaid (20%)
A plaid pattern using two colors—either white and black or the same color in different shades—alternating like a chess board.
Other terms: buffalo plaid, chessboard.

15 Burberry Plaid (20 percent)
Also called "Haymarket plaid" or "Burberry classic plaid." Initially it was introduced as a lining for Burberry's trench coat in 1924. Currently, the Burberry Plaid is a registered trademark under Burberry Group PLC.

Material: Wool

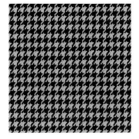

16 Houndstooth Plaid
A plaid pattern that consists of shapes that mimic a dog's teeth.
Other term: dogtooth.

17 Gun Club Plaid
Dual-colored houndstooth plaid

18 Shepherd's Plaid (Border Tartan)
Dyed yarn on white cloth, a small plaid. Inside the black block plaid, you can see a right-slanting white line.

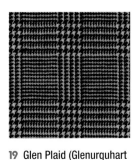

19 Glen Plaid (Glenurquhart Check)
Houndstooth check combined with a thin plaid

Other Patterns

(Dot) Dotted pattern

20 Pindot
The dots are small like a point.

21 Polka Dot
A dotted pattern where the dot is often 0.5 to 1 cm (¼″ to ½″) in diameter

22 Coin Dot
Dot pattern with a coin-sized dot

23 Spot
Bigger than a coin dot

24 Floral Prints (20 percent)
Various designs can be made by changing the colors or shapes.

25 Liberty Prints (20 percent)
This print was created by the Liberty Department, established in 1874 in London. The term can also refer to a small floral print mimicking this print. Influenced by the art nouveau movement—the art style that took Europe by storm from the nineteenth century into the twentieth century—this organic floral pattern is distinctive among early floral prints. This print was strongly influenced by Japanese traditional crafts and Ukiyo-e.

26 Paisley (20 percent)
This pattern was originally used for cashmere shawls produced in the Kashmir region of India. At the beginning of the eighteenth century, it was brought back to the town of Paisley in Scotland and then spread around the world.

27 Sheer
General term for a transparent fabric. Including organdy, georgette, voile, and others, these fabrics are lightweight and thin. Silk, cotton, wool, linen, rayon, and polyester are common materials.

28 Jacquard
A weaving pattern that uses a shedding mechanism so you can weave large patterns

29 Chain Print (20 percent)
A chain motif pattern that possesses a high-quality image and dressy feel

30 Embroidery
Needlework done on a fabric surface

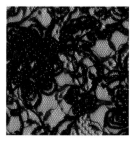

31 Cording
Corded embroidery

Material provided in cooperation with the Takatomi Store at BUNKA GAKUEN

Leather

The treated skin of an animal. A large animal's pelt is called hide; a small animal's pelt is called skin.
Leather is created by tanning, which keeps the pelt from spoiling. A large animal's tanned pelt is called leather, and a small animal's tanned pelt is called skin.

Animal Leather / Domestic Animal Leather

Cow

1 Slink
Among leathers made from very young calves, slink is the top-quality leather. It is glossy and very beautiful. Slink can also be made from horsehide.
Other term: chicken skin.

2 Calfskin
Leather made from a calf that is less than six months old. There are fewer scars, and it has a fine, beautiful texture like velvet. This is a very high-quality leather.

3 Kipskin
Intermediate-grade leather made from calves that are less than one year old. Next to calfskin, this is the smoothest leather.

4 Steerhide
Leather made from an adult male that is more than two years past castration. Tough and durable. Steerhide accounts for 70 percent of all leather production.

Sheep

5 Lambskin
Leather made from a young sheep. It is a soft, thin, lightweight leather that is also durable. This is another popular type of leather.

6 Sheepskin
Leather made form a mature sheep. Fine textured and very strong.

Goat

7 Kidskin
Leather made from a young goat (kid). Thin and soft, but very expensive.

8 Goatskin
Leather made from a mature goat. Thin and very flexible. Usually has small scars, but it is durable and has a high-quality appearance.

Other

Deer

9 Deerskin
Leather made from a deer. Thick and durable, yet soft. It has distinctive crimps.

Pig

10 Pigskin
Leather made from a pig. There is a unique pore pattern on the surface. It breathes well and is quite resistant to friction. Often used as suede.

Bird skin

11 Ostrich
Leather made from an ostrich. After the feather traces are removed, a spiral-like pore appears.

12 Ostrich Leg (20 percent)
Leather made from the legs of an ostrich

Reptile skin

13 Crocodile
Highest-quality skin among reptiles

14 Lizard (20 percent)
Used for high-end bags, wallets, shoes, etc.

15 Iguana
Iguanas mainly live in Latin America. Since they have scales, like a mane, extending from their head to the back of the tail, the abdomen skin is used.

16 Snake
Refers to small snakes. Large snakes are called pythons.

17 Rickrack
A snake's stomach skin

18 Diamond Python (20 percent)
The diamond-shaped scale of a python

19 Baby Python (20 percent)
A small version of the diamond python. It has smaller scales when compared to the diamond python, so it is used to make small items.

Aquatic animal skin

20 Shark
Leather made from a shark's skin. Often used to make small items.

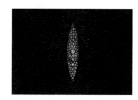

21 Ray (20 percent)
A relative of the shark, rays inhabit tropical, subtropical, and temperate areas of the ocean. The leather is made from a ray's back skin.

Leather finishing and processing

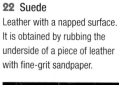

22 Suede
Leather with a napped surface. It is obtained by rubbing the underside of a piece of leather with fine-grit sandpaper.

23 Velour
Velour is created by rubbing the underside of mature cow's leather to create a napped surface. The pile is longer and coarser than suede.

24 Buckskin
A napped surface is created by rubbing the grain side (underside) of a deerskin with sandpaper.

25 Nubuck
A napped surface is created by sanding the grain side of cow leather.

26 Full-Grain Leather
In order create a deep texture and to preserve the leather's grain-side color, full-grain leather is treated with a chrome tanning agent.

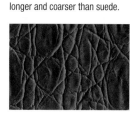

27 Enameled Leather
Coats of synthetic resin create a glossy surface.

28 Embossing Finish
An embossed pattern is created by pressing with heat.

Furs
The original fashion material

1 Mink
A small animal from the Mustelidae family. Very popular among furs because of its durability, mink has beautiful fur with excellent texture. The photo above is sapphire mink.

2 Fox
Fox fur has a wild appearance because of the long and stiff fur. Fur colors are abundant: platinum fox, silver fox, red fox, dyed fox, blue fox, and more. The photo shows blue fox.

3 Rabbit
Rabbit fur has distinctive short and velvety fur.

4 Baby Lamb
The fur from lambs is curled.

5 Lamb
Abundant types are available, from long fur to short and curly.

6 Mouton
Processed lambs' curled fur that has been sheared short

7 Coyote
A relative of the wolf. Has a stiff, wild fur.

8 Weasel
Similar to mink but lacking in suppleness and luster

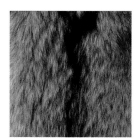

9 Karakul Lamb
A distinct type of lamb from China. Its curly white fur is quite distinctive. It has a slightly short and soft fur, but it lacks luster.

10 Squirrel
Squirrels have short and soft fur that is very lightweight. The best-quality squirrel fur is called loris, and it is produced in Russia. Its beautiful contrasts of blue gray and white make it very attractive.

11 Nutria
Nutria means "weasel fur" in Italian. Originally produced in Latin America.

12 Fake Fur
A fabric made to mimic furs. Other term: faux fur.

Animal Prints

The fashion industry takes inspiration from the appearance of many kinds of animals, replicating their spots, stripes, and markings on various types of textiles.

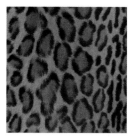

13 Leopard
Its black circular pattern is quite distinctive.

14 Zebra
It has iconic black and white stripes.

15 Holstein
A breed of cow. It is distinctive because of its black spots on white.

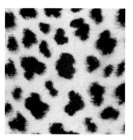

16 Dalmatian
A breed of dog. It has a characteristic white-and-black pattern.

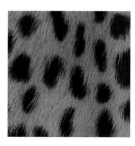

17 Cheetah
The base of the photo is nutria.

Fur Prints

The fur print is a processing method that was employed to make cheap furs look better. However, in recent years, the fur print has come be utilized as a design in itself. So, design possibilities are now nearly endless.

18 Plaid
The base of the photo is pastel mink.

19 Plaid
The base of the photo is pearl mink.

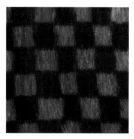

20 Plaid
The base of the photo is blue iris mink.

Material Cooperation: Purchasing Department of Bunka Fashion College

Chapter4
Fashion Design
Expressions

In this section we will consider fashion design presentation methods.

Pictures that are specifically drawn to convey your garment's conceptual design to others are called design drawings. There are two main types.

Design drawing (fashion flat, presentation drawing): These are "portraits" drawn to convey the design aspect of the clothing. Since this particular type of drawing depicts a person wearing clothes, it can suggest not only the shape of those clothes but also their styling (or how they are to be worn).

Item drawing (hanger illustration, working drawing, line drawing): This is a "two-dimensional drawing" that depicts the design and structure of each garment in detail. They are either front style (FS) and back style (BS).

Item drawings have been covered in chapter 2, "Design Ideas," so we will discuss only design drawings here.

Section 1 Design Sketches as Blueprints

Design sketches are used by apparel makers to definitively convey the form of the clothing and feel of the clothing when it is worn. When you draw a design sketch there are three main points: the body, the clothes, and the color/shading. Let's now consider each of these elements.

Body (Proportions)

In this world, clothes are most suited to fashion models. The balanced body used in a fashion design sketch uses these models as a reference point. What type of figure do fashion models have? Let's take a look.

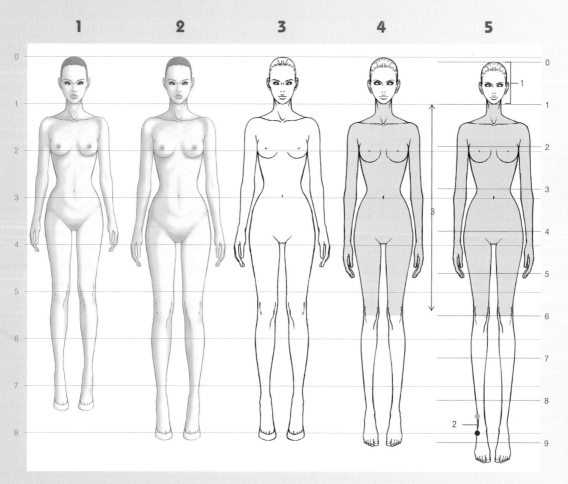

1 The face is 10 percent smaller than the standard eight-heads-tall body.
2 The ankles are shifted down to 8.
3 The pink section is where the clothing will be worn. This section does not change much between a model and a regular person. If we are out of balance here, we will not be able to produce clothing that is exactly like the design sketch, so whether the body is eight heads tall (like a regular person) or nine heads tall (like a sketch model), it is important that we not tamper with the balance of the section where the clothing will be worn.

Pose In fashion design sketching, the only pose is the standing pose. It is not necessary to draw all the details of a model's daily life as manga artists do—for instance, scenes where the model is eating or running. Also, since the face is always viewed at eye level, it is never necessary to change the pose to a bird's-eye view or a low-angle view. So, if you just keep in mind the position of the joints and preserve the correct form of the individual parts that join these joints together, you will be able to sketch a beautiful pose every time. Then, you will find that your overall design ability improves as you make separate sketches of the silhouette (length and width) on the basis of the pose sketch.

Joint positions for a body that is nine heads tall. Each ● is a joint.

1 The median line. The trunk. This line goes straight through the middle of the body. It is an important line for centering the front of the clothing.
2 Front neck point
3 Waistline
4 Hipline
5 The perpendicular line dropped from the front neck point is the center-of-gravity line. When the model is walking, each foot is on this line.

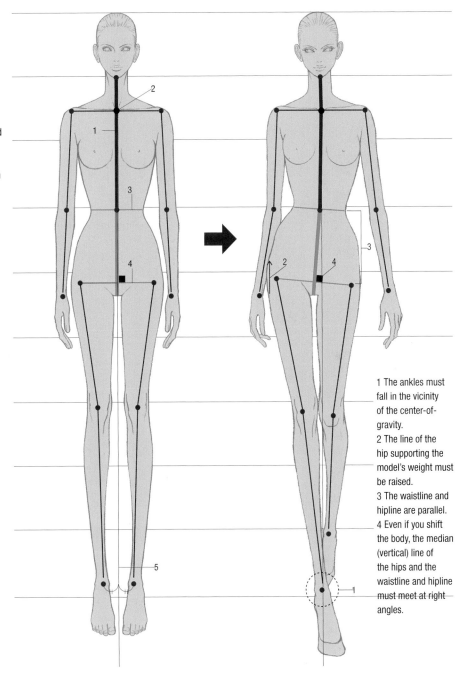

1 A traced silhouette of a normal person's figure between seven and eight heads tall
2 The traced fashion model figure silhouette is eight heads tall. Compared to a normal person, the arms and legs are longer and the face is smaller. This balance highlights the clothing rather than the model. The illustration used here is accurately taken from an actual model's figure, but it probably looks slightly plump. When we look at a three-dimensional figure on a flat plane, it appears fatter than it really is.
3 If a line drawing of a fashion model's figure has no shading, it looks even fatter.
4 Even fashion design sketches that have only a little shading on an eight-heads-tall body make for a slimmer silhouette, while still maintaining the model's overall balance.
5 The nine-heads-tall body. This places emphasis on the clothing. The eight-heads-tall body style is still applied. The numbers assigned to the positions of the basic parts used to draw the nine-heads-tall body, such as the joints and bustline, match up exactly with the newly sized head OR come right in the middle of the eight-heads-tall numbers, so a balanced version of this type of body is easy to draw. (For example, the bust is still at the eight-heads-tall ②, the crotch at ④, and the knees exactly halfway between ⑤ and ⑥, etc. However, when you draw in nine divisions, as seen here, the standard positions do not match up with the numbered lines anymore.)

1 The ankles must fall in the vicinity of the center-of-gravity.
2 The line of the hip supporting the model's weight must be raised.
3 The waistline and hipline are parallel.
4 Even if you shift the body, the median (vertical) line of the hips and the waistline and hipline must meet at right angles.

Making the Pose

Changing the starting point of each joint creates the "movement" of the various parts. It is said that the "center leg pose" (which includes the walking pose), in which one leg is supporting the weight of the entire body, is the most beautiful. This pose has the following two characteristics:

1 The waistline of the supporting leg is always lifted and tilted.
2 When the full body weight is supported on one leg, the center-of-gravity line is always in the vicinity of the ankle of the supporting leg.

Fitting

Clothes are fitted to match the movement and orientation of the body. Make sure that you center the front of the clothing on the median line of the body.

Tops: It is important to think about the range of motion of the arms and leave space around the shoulders and underarms. However, when there are no sleeves, the underarms can fit snuggly.
Bottoms: Fit the bottoms to match the movement of the hips. The grain should be at right angles to the waistline.
So, let's fit some clothing that was designed in chapter 2, no. 3: "Creative Designs: Inspiration from Paintings" (pp. 105 and 106).

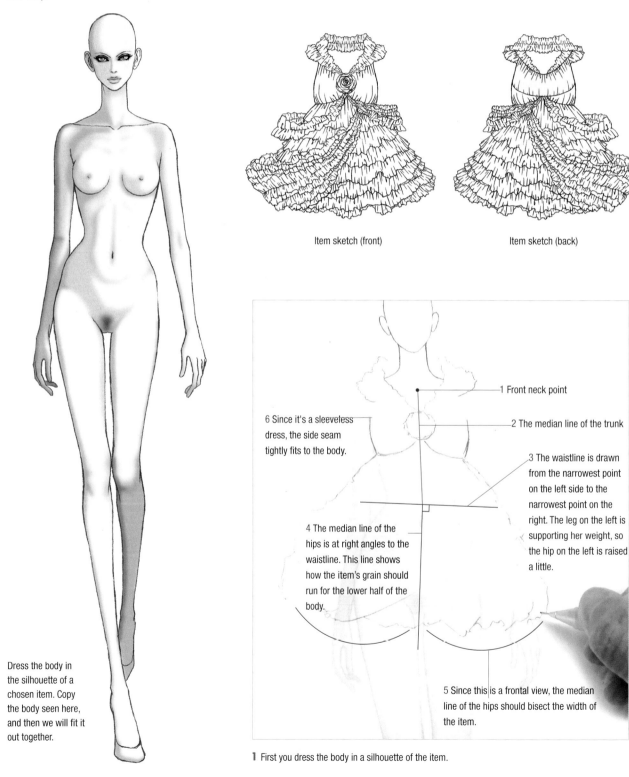

Item sketch (front)

Item sketch (back)

Dress the body in the silhouette of a chosen item. Copy the body seen here, and then we will fit it out together.

1 Front neck point

2 The median line of the trunk

3 The waistline is drawn from the narrowest point on the left side to the narrowest point on the right. The leg on the left is supporting her weight, so the hip on the left is raised a little.

6 Since it's a sleeveless dress, the side seam tightly fits to the body.

4 The median line of the hips is at right angles to the waistline. This line shows how the item's grain should run for the lower half of the body.

5 Since this is a frontal view, the median line of the hips should bisect the width of the item.

1 First you dress the body in a silhouette of the item.

2 Next, draw in the details of the item.

3 Large and small belts of oblique frills are the key design point for this item.

4 Carefully draw in the form of each belt one by one while maintaining the overall balance.

5 The tiered hems can be irregular.

6 Draw in details that are finer than the gather, etc.

7 Come up with a hairstyle.

8 After you have drawn the silhouette, you can put in the flow of the hair.

9 Draw a frilled scrunchie around the arm like a bracelet.

10 The finished product

Shading

Since apparel makers rarely add detailed coloring and patterns to their sketches, unless it is an illustration made for a presentation, let's just consider how to put in shading for the moment. The major benefit of shading is that when you add it to your sketch, the details rise up out of the page and the design becomes clearer. Shading can be broken into three main types:

(Emphasize Contours) Add shading parallel to the contour lines of each "tube."

(The Parts That Stand Out)

A one-piece dress has only one "tube," so you can choose to shade either the left or right contour line. Here the light source is set up facing the body and slanting in from the upper right side, so the lower and left contours are shaded.

The body has one "tube" from the face down to the lower trunk. The arms and legs then make up the other "tubes." Each should be shaded.

Other than the seams, the overall lines of the clothing should be thought of as being three-dimensional and shaded accordingly.
Example: The armhole line: This is a seam, so it is not entirely shaded.
The line that makes up the flare of the dress: This is not a seam; it is a line that expresses the three-dimensional aspect of the dress. Therefore it is shaded.

The following parts are shaded: the body, the nose, the chest, below the knee of the rear leg, etc.

(Wrinkles)

Shading is added to the bottom-left side of wrinkle lines. The deeper the wrinkle, the bigger the shaded area.

In order to express the smooth aspect of the human body, I added neutral tinting.

Here I added bright spots/ glints (the portions without any shading). The light source is on the upper right, so the bright spots/glints should all be on the right side.

Color Variations

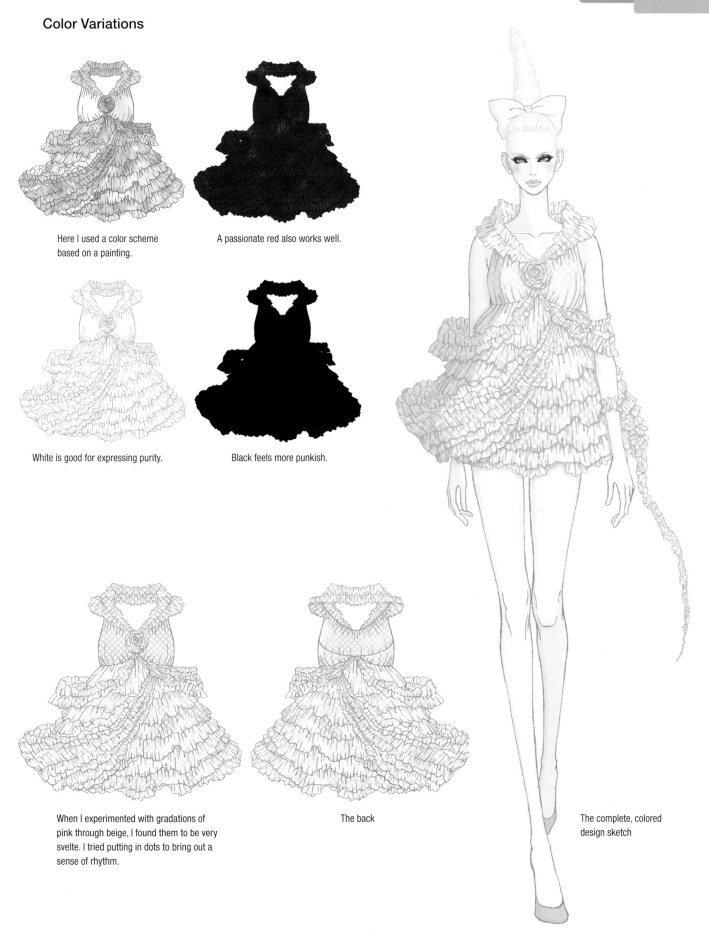

Here I used a color scheme based on a painting.

A passionate red also works well.

White is good for expressing purity.

Black feels more punkish.

When I experimented with gradations of pink through beige, I found them to be very svelte. I tried putting in dots to bring out a sense of rhythm.

The back

The complete, colored design sketch

When you look at a design sketch prepared for a fashion show or a contest, you will notice distinct differences from a design sketch that can be found at an apparel company that deals in clothes. Since its role as a clothing design blueprint and its details are less significant, the design sketch for a fashion show or contest places emphasis on expressing the **image** and essence of the design.

In apparel companies that employ a system of division of labor, design sketches that accurately describe clothing specifics are required so that patternmakers and MDs can understand them. By contrast, if you are the only one directing or producing the design sketches, from the beginning of a fashion show or contest to the end, then—more than simply conveying the structure and details of some clothing—your design sketches need to be appealing through the intensity of their images, their worldview, and their design essence.

When I asked the judges of a particular contest for their opinion, one judge said that a design sketch where he can imagine the finished product in just one glance doesn't actually pique his interest. In other words, a design sketch that piques one's curiosity with thoughts along the lines of "What on earth is that?" and "How does that produce actual clothing?" will stand out among countless entries and have the desired effect on your judges. Having said that, in addition to drawing a design sketch that precedes your image, the most effective method for describing the image and essence of your design is the "fashion croquis."

The croquis can be produced in a short amount of time and is the preferred method for expressing the essence of your target image quickly. The key is to capture the rhythm within the overall target object, thus producing a good first impression. This makes the croquis best suited for contests. One important note regarding the fashion croquis is that you can extract just the important points and the essence of your design while removing portions of the design that can be easily imagined, all without overrendering. You can "draw" a sketch of your image in your head, and then, once your image is complete, you can transfer it onto paper in a short amount of time.

Sample

Drawing a Fashion Croquis

A fashion croquis is a bold technique that captures your target object as a whole. However, if you jump into immediately drawing your ideas on a blank piece of paper, you might struggle.

So, we will begin with precise explanations that follow the croquis steps in order.

Precision Drawing

At first, carefully observe the silhouette and details where they are most distinctive. Then begin to precisely draw. Be sure to thoroughly capture the shadows cast on your target. Refer to p. 128 for shading. Create your shadows by following the three sections labeled "Emphasize Contours," "The Parts That Stand Out," and "Wrinkles." Assume that the source of light is coming from the upper right corner.

1 Make a photocopy of the illustration on p. 127. Add shading to the copy. Draw while holding your pencil at an angle and gently forcing the lead onto your paper.

2 Rub a cotton swab over the image to create subtle shading. Neatly erase anything that juts out too much.

3 After repeating this process, your image should look like this.

Converting Shading to Black and White

In order to emphasize the overall silhouette, we need to create a black-and-white image (no gray scale) and make a template for your fashion croquis.

Scan the drawing with Photoshop and convert the scanned image to black and white (select "Adjustment" under "Image" and then click "Threshold").
The image becomes sharper and more defined.

Fashion Croquis Practice

Dilute an opaque watercolor with clean water. The most suitable density is something like Japanese sumi ink.

Prepare some A4-size paper and draw a vertical line in a single stroke. If you have the proper density of ink, the lower quarter of your line should become scratchy. It is important to load your brush with plenty of paint.

Draw a thick line by holding your brush at an angle. Press the brush down firmly and draw using the middle of the brush. You should press down, draw the line, press, and release, so to speak.

Draw a thin line by holding the brush vertically. Draw by lightly using only the tip of the brush. You should gently press down, lightly draw the line, gently press, and softly release, so to speak.

The Three Techniques of Fashion Croquis

Fashion croquis can be created using three different techniques, all depending on how you capture the silhouette.
You will surely discover your own style while utilizing these techniques.

Shading: technique for painting ¼ of an object
Filling: technique for painting ¾ of an object
Mixture: technique that combines the above two techniques

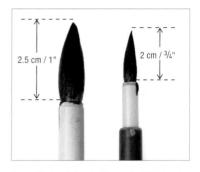

Use a thin brush for shading and a thick brush for filling. Draw a fashion croquis on B4-size paper, using these brushes.

Shading

Since your blank space is quite large, you should be able to express many finite details.

Practice

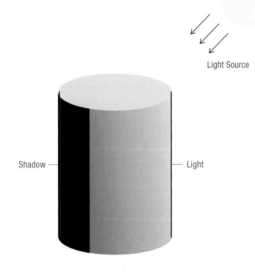

Light Source

Shadow — — Light

Since the human body is essentially a composite cylinder, we should think about how shading works on an actual cylinder. The shadow will be cast on the left, so we need to draw a thick line on the left side that fills ¼ of the cylinder's plane.

1 Draw a thick line on the shaded side for the contour line.

2 Decide on the width of your cylinder.
*Since the source of light is in the upper right corner, the lower line of the contour is thicker.

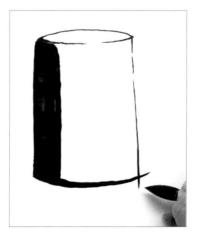

3 Draw the contour where light hits a little thinner. The ratio between the thick and thin lines is 10:1.

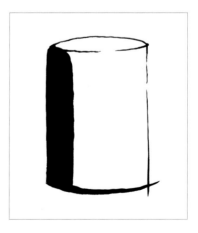

4 The thickness of the two lines (light and shadow) may accidentally become the same when you are mastering the technique. However, once you are able to easily render different thicknesses, you will be able to draw really cool fashion croquis. So, be sure to practice this technique until you master it.

Let's Draw Using Shading

Body

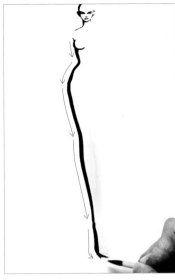

2 Draw each element one by one. Draw rhythmically from the torso, hips, thighs, knees, and legs. A key point is to draw between the joints in one go.

1 Since drawing from scratch requires a lot of work, you need to practice laying down precise lines (refer p.126). To do so, I used a see-through layout pad. Begin with the face. Draw as if you are filling the portion where there is a shadow.

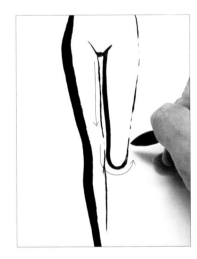

3 Connect the lines between the collarbone and arms, since they work together.

4 Shadows are cast on the model's left knee because the model is walking. Just draw until the knee and stop there.

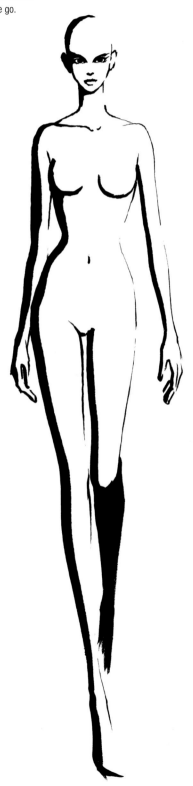

5 Lay the brush down at an angle and draw the shape of the knee with a thick line. Adjust the thickness by laying down and then lifting the brush.

6 The body is complete after drawing the left arm.

Fitting

1 In the same manner, draw the garment over top of the precision drawing. First, add shadows to emphasize the contours: thick on the left and thin on the right.

2 Add details. Considering the fact that the source of light is located in the upper right corner, you should draw each element so that the lower left corner is thicker.

2 Rhythmically brush in the tiers.

4 Once the garment is done, add the body. Then, draw the hair and a ribbon.

5 Complete

(Application)

Use different colors on the garment and the body.
Obviously, the image became sharper and more defined.

Coloring brings out the sharpness of the image.
Feel free to experiment.

Filling Since there is barely any blank space, it can be said that this technique is what accounts for the silhouette the most.

Light Source

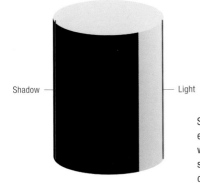

Shadow — Light

Since the human body is essentially a composite cylinder, we should think about how shading works on an actual cylinder. The shadow will be cast on the left, so we don't draw anything on the right ¼ of the cylinder's plane.

1 Fill in the shaded part. Since the plane is large, it cannot be drawn with a single brushstroke. Move the brush up and down while holding it at an angle. The key is to not lift the brush until you finish filling.

2 Decide the width of the shaded area.

3 Thinly draw the lighted contour line.

4 The ratio of the thick and thin lines is 20:1. The contrast is quite strong. This creates a greater impact.

Let's Use Fill to Draw   Body

1 Since drawing from scratch requires a lot of work, you need to practice laying down precise lines (refer p.126). To do so, I used a see-through layout pad. Begin with the face. You should fill most of the space by using the middle of the brush.

2 Draw each element one by one. Draw rhythmically from the torso to the hips, the thighs, the knees, and the legs. Fill the areas between the joints in one go. Add thin lines later.

3 The arms are thin. Draw them in a single stroke while trying not to press the brush down too firmly.

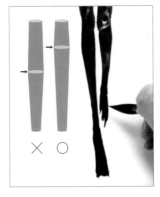

4 You can make the legs look longer by making the highest part of the kneecap really high.

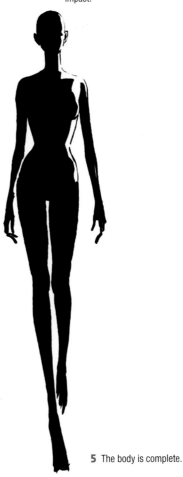

5 The body is complete.

Fitting

1 Draw your garment over the precision drawing in the same manner. First, add shadows to emphasize contours. For the frills, draw them rhythmically as if you were thumping the paper. Thump the paper with more force for the large frills and more gently for the small frills.

2 Continue drawing. Don't fill everything in completely. Make the details somewhat more noticeable by inserting gaps.

3 Add the body once you are done drawing the garment.

4 Then, draw the hair and the ribbon.

5 Complete

(Application)

 Use different colors on the garment and the body.
Obviously, the image became sharper and more defined.

 Coloring brings out a certain sharpness in the image.
Feel free to experiment at this point.

Mixture   The foundational idea here is to "fill" and then apply "shading" to sharpen the image.

Practice

1 We are using opaque watercolors that allow us to paint pale colors over deep colors.

2 Make sure that the topcoat is slightly thicker.

3 First, apply the paint once. Be sure to paint quickly, because the initial coats of paint will become soluble if you paint over it again and again.

4 Apply another coat of color if the undercoat is still visible.

5 Once filling is done, proceed with shading.

6 Add more shadows.

7 Complete

Compare your design sketch (*left*) and your fashion croquis (*right*) of your image. Obviously the fashion croquis is more striking.

Let's Draw Using the Mixture Technique

This technique employs a lot of black for shading. This will bring out a fair amount of sharpness.

Variations

In the sample illustration below, we toned down the color of the
shadows and added dots on the dress and ribbon.

1 Here we made the body a "precise
drawing." It increases the impact on
the garment drawn using the "mixture"
technique.

Let's try more drawing by
combining various patterns. Feel
free to create your own patterns
and acquire your own
unique design style.

2 Color Variation 1
By employing the filling technique on
the body and the mixture technique on
the other elements, we emphasized the
three-dimensional feel of the garment. In
order to make a translucent white item
striking, you must use a dark color for the
background.

3 Color Variation 2
Paint the body by using the "mixture"
technique, but using an increased ratio
of white. Also, paint the item by using the
"filling" technique with an increased ratio
of black. By doing so, you will emphasize
the garment and create a more punkish
image. Here, we attempted to bring out
contrast by making the background pink.

Chapter5
The Process of Creating a Fashion Illustration

From "Design Conception" to "Rough Sketch"

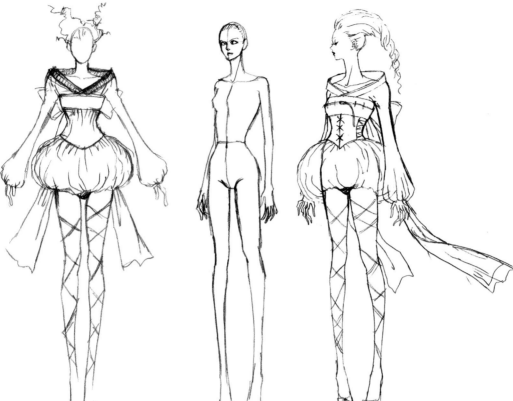

1 Let's take a look at the process for drawing a fashion illustration of a garment created under the theme of "kimono" from p. 5. First of all was the design conception. There are various arrangements for kimono; however, I felt that a skirt that is shorter than the inner is rare, so I decided to incorporate that into this concept. The fashion croquis method is suitable for designs with striking silhouettes. I was conscious of this and sought to bring out the sharpness to the silhouette.

2 In thinking about the pose, I decided that I wanted the sash at the back to stand out. So, I decided on a diagonal pose.

3 The rough sketch is complete once the garment is on the body. I came up with an interesting idea for the hair, so I made the head look sideways in order to show off the hairstyle.

From "Painting" to "Scanning with Photoshop" and "Making the Drawing Lines Transparent"

4 Place your layout pad over the rough sketch and draw your fashion croquis. I applied the "shading" technique to the whole drawing. Once you are finished with your fashion croquis, start Photoshop (CS5) and prepare to scan the fashion croquis. Under "File," select "Import." Then, choose which scanner you will use.
Color: Grayscale / Resolution: 400dpi

5 After scanning, I noticed that the image had an uneven tone. So, I made some adjustments. Under "Image," I selected "Adjustments" and then clicked on "Levels."

6 You can clear up the contrast by dragging the slider left or right. The trick here is to drag the slider over the black mountain.

7 After the level adjustments are done

8 Make the background transparent.

1 Bring out the Layer Palette. Under "Window," select "Layers."

2 Click on the box located at the top right of the palette. Select "Duplicate Layer" and create a copy of the background.

3 Click on the Magic Wand Tool (the stick with the *) in the Toolbox and then click on the white part of the copy of the background.

4 Select the entire white part. Under "Select," click "Similar."

5 Delete all the white area by pressing the delete key.

6 Delete the original drawing lines. In the palette, click on the name listed in "Background" layer. Click "Select" and then "All." Press the delete key to delete.

7 Double-click on the name of the "Background Copy" layer and enter the new name "Line."

Click the Show/Hide Checkbox (the eye icon) on the "Background" layer to hide, and make sure that only the drawing line is visible.

"Separating into Parts"

9 Select the hair by using the Lasso Select Tools.

10 Under "Select," click on "Edit in Quick Mask Mode." The red area is the portion that is not selected.

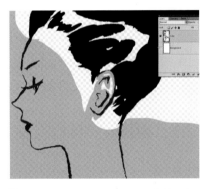

11 Since the ear area is selected, it is filled in using the Brush tool.

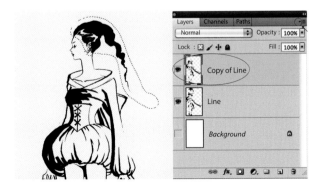

12 Click on "Select" and click on "Edit in Quick Mask Mode" to restore the display. Then, click on the box located at the top right on the Layer Palette. Select "Duplicate Layer" to create "a copy of Line." Then, press the delete key to erase the hair part.

13 Click on the name on the "Line" layer. Create a layer just for the hair part by clicking "Select" and then "Reverse." Then press the delete key.

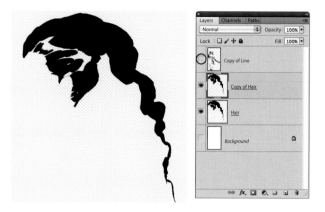

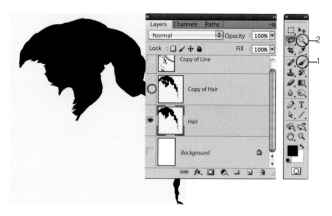

14 Give the name "Hair" to the duplicate of the layer. Hide the other layers by clicking the Show/Hide Checkbox (the eye icon) so that only the "Hair" layer is visible on the screen.

15 Next, hide a copy of the Hair layer by clicking Show/Hide Checkbox (the eye icon) and then click on the name of the "Hair" layer in the Palette. Fill in the blank area by using the Brush tool.

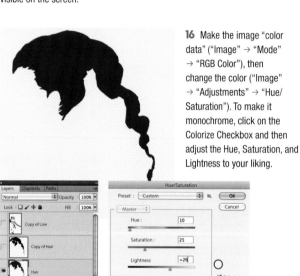

16 Make the image "color data" ("Image" → "Mode" → "RGB Color"), then change the color ("Image" → "Adjustments" → "Hue/Saturation"). To make it monochrome, click on the Colorize Checkbox and then adjust the Hue, Saturation, and Lightness to your liking.

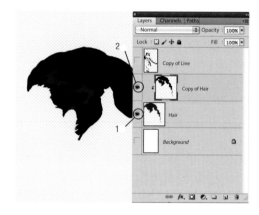

17 Select the copy of the Hair layer by clicking on the name displayed in the Layers Palette. Then, click on the Show/Hide Checkbox (the eye icon) to make the layer visible. And then, select "Create Clipping Mask" under the "Layer" menu. By doing so, the layer indicated with 1 is the color of the "plane," and the layer indicated with 2 is the color of the "shadow or lines." You can separate all the parts by repeating this process.

> **From "Color Coordination" to "Setting Pattern"**

18 The photo above shows the image after a Clipping Mask has been created for each of the parts separated into a plane layer and a shadow (line) layer. For example, since the small belt is drawn over the wide belt, the belt1 layer is located above the belt2 layer. Click the Show/Hide Checkbox (the eye icon) of the "Background" layer in order to restore it to white.

19 Adjust each of the colors by selecting "Image," clicking on "Adjustments" and then selecting "Hue/Saturation." For a colored image, drag the slider to adjust without checking "Colorize."

142

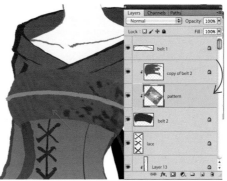

21 On the Layers Palette, drag the "pattern" layer and move it between the plane layer and the shadow layer. The shadow layer hides the pattern (see blue arrow).

22 Change Blending Mode from "Normal" to "Multiple" in order to make the pattern visible. By repeating this process, you can add color coordination and pattern.

20 A separately created pattern can be inserted. First, open and copy the file that contains the pattern that you intend to insert. Click "Select," click on "All" and then on "Edit," and then select "Copy."
Return to the file of the illustration and select "Edit." Click on "Paste" and name the file "pattern."

Makeup

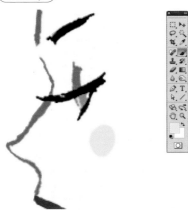

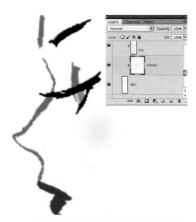

25 Complete. The other illustrations on pp. 4 and 5 are also drawn using this same method.

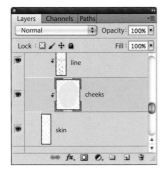

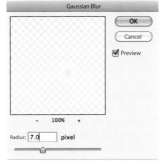

23 Draw in some blush. Create a new layer ("cheeks") in between the skin's plane ("skin") layer and line ("line") layer. It is a clipping mask. Then, draw a circle by using the Brush Tool.

24 Set the radius at 7 pixels. Select "Filter," click on "Blur," then select "Gaussian Blur."
In a same manner, you can draw eyeshadow, using the Brush Tool, and then blur that as well.

143

Afterword

Seeking brand-new designs all the time and conveying them to others in your own style is a difficult task. If there is one main tip to increasing your ability to conceive of new ideas, I think that it would be to not have stereotypes. If you fixate on one-sided ideas, you won't allow yourself to expand upon the multifaceted ideas that are floating around in your head.

In order to have feelings such as "Wow, that's interesting!" or "Oh, that's new!," it is important not to be bound by your past successes. In other words, you wouldn't wear the same clothes all the time after receiving a simple compliment of "That looks good on you." It can be difficult to let go of a compliment you once received, but remember that fashion means "keep going forward."

Here are some things to keep in mind. For a fashion designer, what does l'air du temps mean? Briefly, it is something that "has not existed before." It is a style, or an item, that wasn't around until now—because something new is created every year. Fashion keeps evolving. Therefore, it is crucial to recognize things that you have not seen before. There might be a style that has been seen before, but the overall balance has changed—or an item that was popular in the past but now has different material. You must be certain to effectively recognize such small changes. Moreover, it is important to understand the answer to the question "Why is such fashion popular now?" while remaining cognizant of current issues—this is the ability to read l'air du temps.

That ability is nurtured from thoroughly learning the fundamentals of fashion—silhouettes of clothes, details, materials, methods of presentation, and more. Do not pursue this study in some vague manner; you must carefully observe and understand the fundamentals that will help you. I truly wish you the best of luck!

Last but not least, I would like to thank all the people who always gave me inspiration—all of the students I met and all those I met through my work. Thank you all so very much.

—Zeshu Takamura
October 16, 2010 / April 27, 2023

About the Author

Zeshu Takamura is a fashion illustrator and fashion style researcher. A professor of fashion science at Tokyo's Bunka Gakuen University and its graduate school, he is the director of the division of fashion graphics. He is a graduate of Tokyo Gakugei University and Kuwasawa Design School and previously served as a lecturer at Tokyo's Mode Gakuen and other institutions. Takamura has shared his research and knowledge on fashion design and illustration through several books, including *Fashion Design Techniques: The Basics and Practical Application of Fashion Illustration* (Schiffer, 2016). His books have been translated into English, French, and other languages.

Other Schiffer Books by the Author:
Fashion Design Techniques: The Basics and Practical Application of Fashion Illustration, 978-0-7643-5047-4

Copyright © 2023 by Schiffer Publishing, Ltd.

FASHION DESIGN ARCHIVE
© 2011 Zeshu Takamura
© 2011 GRAPHIC-SHA PUBLISHING CO., LTD
This book was first designed and published in Japan in 2011 by Graphic-sha Publishing Co., Ltd.
This English edition was published in 2023 by Schiffer Publishing, Ltd.
English translation rights arranged with GRAPHIC-SHA PUBLISHING CO., LTD
through Japan UNI Agency, Inc., Tokyo

Original edition creative staff:
Book design: Yamaguchi Shingo Design room (Yoji Ebihara, Naoki Kanaoka, Yusuke Tagiku)
Editing: Mari Nagai
Foreign edition production and management: Takako Motoki (Graphic-sha Publishing Co., Ltd.)

Library of Congress Control Number: 2023931234

Cover design by Christopher Bower
Type set in Helvetica Neue/Bauhaus/DIN

ISBN: 978-0-7643-6677-2
Printed in China

Published by Schiffer Publishing, Ltd.
4880 Lower Valley Road
Atglen, PA 19310
Phone: (610) 593-1777; Fax: (610) 593-2002
Email: info@schifferbooks.com
Web: www.schifferbooks.com

FSC
www.fsc.org
MIX
Paper from
responsible sources
FSC® C167893